THE GOSPELS: SIMPLY EXPLAINED

•

Rev. Jude Winkler, OFM Conv.

CATHOLIC BOOK PUBLISHING CORP.
New Jersey

IMPRIMI POTEST: Michael Kolodziej, OFM Conv.
Minister Provincial of St. Anthony of Padua Province (USA)
NIHIL OBSTAT: Rev. Donald E. Blumenfeld, Ph.D.
   Censor Librorum
IMPRIMATUR: ✠ Most Rev. John J. Myers, J.C.D., D.D.
   Archbishop of Newark

(T-668)

ISBN 978-0-89942-714-0

Dedication

To Dad and Mom

Matthew

Mark

Luke

John

CONTENTS

Introduction

L ATE in the first century A.D., four evangelists sat down and produced four accounts of the mission of Jesus. Each of them had a particular perspective on what Jesus said and did because each was writing for a different audience. Matthew was writing for a Jewish Christian community that had been persecuted and exiled from the synagogue. He showed how Jesus was the Messiah Whom Yahweh had sent into the world and how the Church was the New Israel. Mark wrote for a mixed audience in Rome that was undergoing persecution. His Jesus is dirty and dusty, just off the road. He teaches the community that was being martyred that they would meet Jesus in their sufferings. Luke wrote for a more educated Greek-speaking audience. His Jesus is filled with mercy and compassion, reaching out to those who needed Him most. John wrote for a community that was highly spiritual. His Gospel presents Jesus as an enlightened spiritual guide Who is truly God and man.

When we hear the Gospel proclaimed in the liturgy, we often don't notice the name of the evangelist who wrote that particular account. Because of this, we can miss some of the underlying messages that each evangelist added to his account. This book was written to provide a basic introduction to each of the four Gospels and to show their similarities and differences. It is not a verse by verse study, but rather is intended to provide an overview for those who wish to read the Gospels within the context in which they were written.

If one has not yet studied the Gospels, it is possible that some of the insights contained in this book will be challenging or confusing. My recommendation is that you read and reread what is being said, but even more important, that you bring it to prayer. Any study of the Gospels should lead us to fall on our knees and pray to the God Who loves us so much that He would send His only Son into this world out of love for us. May the Holy Spirit, Who inspired these holy accounts of the life and ministry of Jesus, inspire your hearts as well.

Shalom,
Fr. Jude Winkler, OFM Conv.

Part I

The Gospel of Matthew

Chapter 1

Who, When and Why

EACH of the four Gospels had a particular point of view. They all present the story of Jesus and His ministry. They all speak about the same events, but each one was written for a different community with its own particular needs.

Mark presents the basic story of Jesus as the Son of Man Who came to suffer and die for us. Luke presents a Jesus Who is filled with compassion and wisdom. John speaks of Jesus as a spiritual guide Who reveals the secrets of God.

Matthew is the most Jewish of the Gospels. It presents Jesus as the new Moses for the new Israel. It shows how Jesus fulfilled the prophecies of the Old Testament concerning the coming Messiah. Who was Matthew? Why did he write his Gospel? For whom did he write it? What are his main themes?

Who Wrote the Gospel?

TRADITION tells us that Matthew, the tax collector, wrote the first Gospel in Aramaic. This is why the Gospel is always placed as the first Gospel of the four in the New Testament. Is this tradition reliable?

A first difficulty we face is that we do not have a copy of the original Aramaic version. We only have the Greek version, which is the one we translate into our modern languages. Furthermore, when scholars examined the Greek version, they determined that it was not translated from Aramaic. One can almost always tell if a work is a translation or if it was originally written in that language. This Gospel was written in Greek. There are, for example, word plays in Greek that are obviously not translated from Aramaic. There are just no Aramaic words that could make the same word play.

A second difficulty is that the Gospel of Matthew often quotes the Old Testament to show that Jesus is the Messiah. Yet, Matthew was a tax collector and that was considered to be an unclean profession. How could a tax collector have known the Old Testament well enough to make all of these citations? It doesn't make sense.

A third difficulty involves this Gospel's relationship to the Gospel of Mark. It is obvious that one of these authors used the other's Gospel as one of his sources. They have over 600 verses in common. Mark's Gospel is short and relatively poorly written. Matthew is much longer and it is very well written. Does it make sense to go from a short, poorly written Gospel and to add to the material and correct the grammar to make it a longer, better written Gospel or vice versa?

Given all of these problems, it is difficult to sustain the tradition that Matthew, the tax collector, wrote this particular version of the Gospel. Yet, ancient traditions should not be discarded carelessly. Is there something in the tradition that can be preserved?

Quite some time ago, scholars noticed that there were certain verses contained in Matthew that also appear in Luke but do not appear in Mark. Scholars called these verses "Q" (from the German word "Quelle," a word that means "the source"). These verses are sayings of Jesus. They are obviously translated into Greek from Aramaic. They speak about the end of the world as if it was going to happen very soon. When during the history of the Church did people believe that the end of the world was close at hand? It was at the beginning of the Church. In the Old Testament, the resurrection of the dead was considered to be a sign of the end times. When Jesus rose from the dead, early Christians considered it to be the beginning of the end times. Paul even told people in Corinth that they should not get married so that they could do the work of the Lord while they prepared for the return of Jesus. It was only later in history that Christians realized that the end times might not be coming soon. They stopped saying that it was at hand and began to say that it was coming like a thief in the night.

So if the verses in Q speak of an imminent return of Jesus in glory, it means that they were probably collected together early in the history of the Church (when that belief was still common). Furthermore, they were originally written in Aramaic, a language that was commonly used in the Church only in its earliest days. Thus, Q must be a collection made early in the history of the Church. Could it have been made by Matthew? This would explain the origin of the tradition that Matthew wrote the first Gospel in Aramaic. The only thing was that it was not a full Gospel; it was only a collection of sayings. These verses were later incorporated into the Gospels of Matthew and Luke.

Second Matthew

THEN who wrote the Gospel of Matthew? Scholars believe that it was written by a converted Pharisee. This would explain the frequent citations from the Old Testament. Pharisees continuously studied Sacred Scripture, so second Matthew, if he had been a Pharisee before he converted, would have known these verses well. We don't know this author's name. It was lost when he incorporated Q into his work. If our theory about the authorship of Q is correct, that Matthew the apostle wrote it, then it would appear that the entire Gospel was named after the author of this one source. Why would this happen? Because Matthew was an apostle, and he therefore possessed apostolic authority. Second Matthew, on the other hand, was a relatively obscure author, and he would not have had that authority. If this Gospel was to be accepted by the universal Church, it needed the authority of an apostle. (Henceforth, we will speak of the author of this Gospel as "Matthew" even if it was actually Second Matthew.)

Matthew used various sources when he put together his Gospel. He used the Gospel of Mark, incorporating almost every verse (although he rearranged their order). He used Q (which we believe was written by the apostle Matthew). He also used another source that we call M. This was his own particular source and its material does not appear in the other Gospels. This is especially the material contained in the infancy narratives at the beginning of the Gospel, the Resurrection narratives at the end of the Gospel, and a number of parables about the coming judgment scattered throughout the Gospel.

Where did Matthew write his Gospel? From the Greek of the Gospel, we can determine that it was probably written in Southern Syria. We know this because even though Greek was spoken throughout most of the eastern part of the Roman Empire, each area had its own peculiarities in pronunciation (which would affect its spelling) and grammar and even the choice of vocabulary (much as English, which is spoken throughout the world, has its own peculiarities in various countries and even regions).

Why Did He Write This Gospel?

WHY did Matthew decide to put together these sources and produce the Gospel of Matthew as we know it? From the apologetic tone of the Gospel (strongly defending Jesus from false accusations and showing quite an aggressive attitude toward the Pharisees), it would seem that it was written at a time of tension and probably even persecution. Furthermore, given the very Jewish tone of the Gospel, the persecution probably did not involve the entire Christian community. It was Matthew's community that was being persecuted, a very traditional Jewish-Christian community.

To understand what was going on, it would be useful to examine what was happening in those days. In the late 60s, the Jewish people of Israel rebelled against their Roman overlords. It was a disastrous episode, for in 70 A.D. the Romans conquered Jerusalem and destroyed the temple. This had been the focal point for Judaism. It was the only place in the world where one could sacrifice an animal and obtain forgiveness for one's sins. Now it was gone.

Before this, Judaism had been quite tolerant in what one could believe and still call oneself a Jew. As long as one believed in the one God of Israel, Yahweh, then one could practice one's faith in any of a number of ways. There were Sadducees. They were very traditional theologically. They only accepted the first five books of the Bible, the Pentateuch, as normative. They did not believe in angels or divine messengers or in the resurrection of the dead. There were Pharisees. They were dedicated laymen who were very rigorous in their observance of the law, but they were also innovative in their theology. They accepted most of the books of the Old Testament. They believed that God had a plan for each person and communicated that will to us through angels and other divine messengers. They also believed in the resurrection of the dead. There were Zealots. These were revolutionaries who were trying to overthrow the Romans. There were Essenes. They were celibate monks who lived by the Dead Sea, preparing themselves for the coming battle between the Sons of Light and the Sons of Darkness. There were even Nazarenes, Jews who believed that Jesus was the Messiah Whom Yahweh had sent.

With the destruction of the temple, the Pharisees, who were now called the rabbis, gathered in Jamnia to determine what it would mean to be a Jew in the future. (Notice that the Sadducees are not mentioned for they ceased to exist as an organized body after the destruction of the temple.) The rabbis formed schools in which they discussed the obligations of the law. These were not schools in the modern sense of the word, for they were more groups of disciples gathered around an important scholar. The main rabbi would propose a question, and the students would discuss the best way to respond to it. This was called the process of binding and loosing, for it was the way by which the rabbis determined what the rules for Judaism would be over the next decades.

During these years, the rabbis made three major decisions. First of all, they decreed that only those books written in Hebrew or Aramaic would be accepted into their canon, the list of books in their Bible. This decision excluded the books that had recently been written in Greek: 1 and 2 Maccabees, Tobit, Judith, Wisdom, Sirach and Baruch as well as some parts of Daniel. That list of books should look somewhat familiar. This is the difference between a Catholic and a Protestant Old Testament. Since most Churches in the early days of the Church spoke Greek, Christians continued to use them even though the rabbis had excluded them. It was only in the 16th century that Martin Luther argued that they should be excluded from the Christian Bible. Catholics call these books Deutero-Canonical while Protestants call the same books Apocrypha. One could make a very good argument that since Jesus seems to have used these very books (for He has allusions to them in His teachings), then they should be considered to be part of the Bible.

A second decision that the rabbis made was to reject the Greek translation of the Old Testament called the Septuagint. This name means "the seventy," for tradition holds that it was translated by seventy-two translators, and even though each translated the text individually, their translations were word for word the same. The reason that the rabbis rejected the Septuagint was that Christians were using some of its translations as proof texts to show that Jesus was the Messiah. The rabbis commissioned new translations that would be more literal, closer to the original Hebrew.

Finally, it was around this time that the rabbis definitively decided to exclude Christians from the synagogue. They did this by adding a prayer to their prayer of the faithful (which they called the Eighteen Benedictions). It basically said, "May heretics die immediately, and may Christians burn in Hell forever." (It is not known if this was the exact original formulation of the prayer, but this seems to be the basic sense of what the prayer said even from its early days.)

If one was suspected of being a Christian, then one was asked to read these prayers. If one refused or hesitated, then one was excluded from the synagogue. This was not simply a question of losing one's place of prayer. A person's family and friends treated that person as if he were dead. One sees an example of this in the play and film "Fiddler on the Roof." The daughter who marries the Christian is treated this way.

But this was not all. In those days, there were only two legitimate religions in the Roman Empire: Judaism and the worship of the emperor. If one was no longer a Jew, then one was expected to burn incense to the emperor. If one refused that, then one was convicted of treason. The rationale behind this is that one was not praying for the safety of the empire in one of the acceptable ways. Thus, to be thrown out of the synagogue was a death sentence. It was also, according to the prayer added to the 18 Benedictions, a condemnation to Hell for all eternity.

This was why Matthew wrote his Gospel (remember, we are actually talking about Second Matthew). He wrote it to console a community that was facing persecution. He also wrote it to demonstrate to Christians that their faith in Jesus was warranted. This explains the apologetic tone of the Gospel, for Matthew wanted to prove the lies being told about Jesus to be false. Furthermore, it explains the vitriolic tone against the Pharisees found in this Gospel. Remember, we believe that Matthew was probably a converted Pharisee, and it was the Pharisees/rabbis who had excluded this community from the synagogue. Matthew shows all the signs of having felt betrayed by his old comrades. They had studied the law of Israel together. Now they had condemned him and his Christian brothers and sisters. For as much as the Gospel of Matthew has sayings about loving our enemies, Matthew does not seem to succeed all that well in doing this.

Questions

1. Why do scholars believe that Matthew, the tax collector, did not write the Gospel of Matthew?
2. Who did write this Gospel?
3. What was the Council of Jamnia? Why and how did the rabbis exclude Christians from the synagogue?

Prayer

Loving God, help me to remember that things are often more complicated than they seem to be. Help me to see Your presence in the often confusing currents of life and to realize that You are always working through these things.

Chapter 2

The Infancy Narrative

The Beginning of the Gospel

HAVING said all of this, we can begin to examine some passages from this Gospel. It begins, "The book of the genealogy of Jesus Christ, the son of David, the son of Abraham." This introduction is a perfect example of how Matthew tries to demonstrate how Jewish Jesus is.

The Gospel starts with the word "genealogy." In Greek, this word sounds very much like the word "Genesis." Matthew chose this word to make an allusion to the Greek name for the first book of the Bible. The message is that this is a new beginning.

This genealogy is the reason why the symbol for Matthew's Gospel is a human being for the genealogy at the beginning of the Gospel presents the human origin of Jesus.

Jesus is called the Christ (the Messiah). He is the son of Abraham. Abraham was the father of the Jews, thus emphasizing the Jewishness of Jesus. (Luke ends his genealogy with Adam to show that Jesus came to save everyone.) Notice that Matthew does not mention Sarah. This is a very Jewish Gospel, and women did not count in Jewish society in those days. All throughout the Gospel of Matthew women play a less significant role than in the other Gospels, e.g. the infancy narrative where Joseph is the central character and not Mary.

Jesus is also called the son of David. Why did Matthew specifically mention David and not one of the other kings of Israel, e.g. Solomon? The reason is that David was considered to be the model of what the Messiah should be. The borders of the kingdom reached their widest extent during his reign for they went from river (the Nile) to river (the Euphrates).

This Davidic nature of the Messiah is reiterated in the fact that the genealogy has three series of fourteen generations. There is a hidden meaning in the number fourteen. The people of Israel had a word game named *gematria*. One took each letter of a word and gave that letter a numeric value. A = 1; B = 2; C = 3, etc. When one arrives at the tenth letter, one begins to jump by 10's, so that j = 10; k = 20; l = 30, etc. One adds up all the numeric values of the letters in a word, and the sum total is the symbolic number that represents that word. An example of this is found in the Book of Revelation. The number 666 is the *gematria* number for "Nero Caesar." The Book of Revelation was thus saying that if one wanted to be evil, then Nero was one's model.

What does the number 14 symbolize? The fourth letter of the Hebrew alphabet is D; the sixth letter of the Hebrew alphabet is V. DVD = 4 + 6 + 4. These are the consonants of the name David (vowels don't count in Hebrew). Thus, Matthew is saying that Jesus is not only like David; He is three times better (fourteen generations, fourteen generations and fourteen generations).

Even the triple mention of David has symbolic meaning. There was no comparative or superlative degree in Hebrew. If one wanted to say "bigger," then one had to say, "big, big." If one wanted to say "biggest," then one had to say, "big, big, big." This is the reason why we repeat things three times at Mass, such as "holy, holy, holy." Matthew is saying that Jesus is the "Davidest." If one liked David, then one would love Jesus.

We know that this is Matthew's intention for he "cooked" the list a bit. He dropped out a few names from the central group of fourteen just so he could have fourteen generations in each section. In genealogies, the actual names of the ancestors were less important than the symbolic meaning presented by the genealogy.

Still, why was the genealogy through Joseph and not Mary? Joseph, after all, wasn't the father of Jesus, God was. But we have to remember that this is a Jewish Gospel in which women don't really count. Furthermore, in those days, people tended to marry rather close relatives. A perfect marriage, according to the rabbis, was when an uncle married a niece. Thus, Joseph and Mary were probably close relatives anyway and the genealogy, even though it is Joseph's, would have been quite similar to Mary's.

Women in the Genealogy

IT has already been stated that this was a Jewish Gospel and women didn't count. This is why women's names were not put into genealogies. That is why it is so odd that we find the names of a number of women in this genealogy. What is even more strange is which women's names are included.

The first woman is Tamar. She was the daughter-in-law of Judah the Patriarch. Her story is messy. After she lost two husbands (both sons of Judah), she was supposed to marry Judah's third son. Judah conspired not to give her his only remaining son by telling her to go back home until his son came of age. Tamar realized what was going on, so she tricked Judah into having sex with her so that she could give her deceased husband a descendant in Israel. Instead of condemning Tamar for adultery or incest, the Bible lauds her for her resourcefulness in fighting for the rights of her deceased husband.

The second woman in this genealogy is Rahab. She was a prostitute in Jericho when the Israelites entered the Promised Land. She hid the two Israelite spies when they came into the city to spy out the defenses. Because of this, she and her family were saved from the fate of the other residents of Jericho when it was conquered by the Israelites.

The third woman was Ruth. She was a truly virtuous woman, but she had the unfortunate background of being a Moabite. Israelites hated the Moabites.

Then there is Bathsheba. Interestingly, Matthew doesn't even use her name. She is called the wife of Uriah the Hittite. This reminds us of the story of her adultery with David and how David conspired to have Uriah killed.

Finally, there is the Blessed Virgin Mary. What is she doing in this neighborhood?

There is a bit of apologetics going on here. Christians claimed that Mary was a virgin and that the father of her child was God Himself. The rabbis rejected and even mocked this belief. There wasn't even a strong tradition in Judaism that the Messiah would be born of a virgin. The rabbis called Jesus "Ben Pantera" in their writings. "Ben" means "the son of" and "Pantera," according to the rabbis, was the name of the Roman soldier who had a fling with Mary. Matthew is attacking this libel by saying that God worked through many unusual women in the past who all became the ancestors of kings of Israel. Couldn't God also work through a virgin from a backwoods town to be the mother of the Messiah?

The Birth of Jesus

AFTER the genealogy, we hear about the birth of Jesus. Notice that there is no account of the annunciation. We simply hear that Mary, a virgin, was betrothed to a man named Joseph when she became pregnant. Betrothal was a type of formal arrangement in which one was considered to be married to the other in everything but actually living together. If Mary were pregnant, then it would have been considered to be a form of adultery.

Joseph was a righteous man. A truly righteous Jewish man would have had his fiancée stoned to death. He did not do this. He was a merciful man, so he decided to divorce her quietly. This was not all that great for Mary, for she would have been considered to be a fallen woman. Yet, she would still be alive. But God took Joseph beyond what he thought was possible. An angel appeared to Joseph in a dream and told Joseph that the Child Mary was carrying had been conceived by the Holy Spirit. Joseph therefore took Mary into his home and cared for her and her child. This account is all the more extraordinary when one considers the fact that the author of this Gospel was probably a converted Pharisee. Pharisees tried to keep the law to the letter. In this text, God was revealing that true righteousness has little to do with keeping the law; it was a question of showing mercy.

Why did Joseph get his revelation from God in a dream? It is because he is named after Joseph, the Patriarch, the dreamer of the Old Testament.

Notice that the Holy Family does not move from Nazareth to Bethlehem in this Gospel. In Matthew, they seem to start out in Bethlehem. When they return from exile in 2:23, they go to Nazareth because they cannot return home (as if they had never before lived in Nazareth). If one takes into account some of the historic difficulties of Luke's account, then we would have to lean toward Matthew being more historic than Luke. The Holy

Family probably lived in Bethlehem at the beginning of the story and only moved to Nazareth after they returned from exile in Egypt. (This would not prevent Jesus being born in a cave for the family was so poor that they very well might have lived in a cave.)

In 1:22, we hear a fulfillment text. Matthew quotes Isaiah 7:14 to show how Mary's being a virgin was foretold by the prophets. The only difficulty with this text is the fact that the original Hebrew form of the verse does not speak of a "virgin." The original Hebrew uses the word "almah" which actually means "young maiden." The prophet Isaiah was probably referring to his own wife, and the son who would be called Emmanuel was his own son (for all of the prophet's sons had symbolic names). The name Emmanuel means "God is with us," and it was to be a reminder to the king to trust in the providence of God.

When this verse was translated into Greek in the Septuagint, the translators used the Greek word "parthenos," which means "virgin." (Remember how the Parthenon in Athens is named after the "virgin goddess," Athena.)

When Matthew wanted to speak of the virginity of Mary, he quoted the Greek version of this verse. This was one of the reasons why the rabbis rejected the Septuagint translation. It was the version that Christians were using to prove that Jesus was the Messiah. We have to be careful here, though, for the fact that the word "virgin" is a mistranslation does not mean that we should doubt Mary's virginity. Matthew knew that she was a virgin, and he was only looking for verses in the Old Testament that had foretold this.

The virginity of Mary is reiterated by the statement in 1:25 that Joseph had no relations with Mary before the child was born. In English, this sounds as if they might have had relations later. That is not the meaning of this verse. It is simply a statement that there was no way that this child could have been Joseph's; the father was God Himself.

People often ask why Joseph would not have had relations with Mary after Jesus was born. Remember, he knew that Jesus was conceived through the power of the Holy Spirit. He knew that Mary was special, a chosen one of God. Isn't it conceivable that he would have said to himself, "hands off," as a way of respecting God's revelation?

Some people have argued that the virginity of Mary was only an example of Christianity's rejection of the flesh and sexuality. The problem with this argument is that Matthew's Gospel was so Jewish. In the Jewish world, virginity was essential for someone who was marrying, but it was not seen as a value in itself. The Jewish attitude toward marriage and sex was very positive and natural. There would have been no reason for a Jewish Christian author to make up this detail in the story, especially since Jewish people did not really expect the Messiah to be born from a virgin (with the sole exception of the Greek version of Is 7:14).

The Magi

AT the beginning of chapter 2, we hear that Magi came from the east to pay homage to the newborn king of the Jews.

Magi were astrologers. They were not the kings as mentioned in the Epiphany song, "We Three Kings of Orient Are." Furthermore, it is not even clear that there were three of them. There are three gifts, which is probably why we speak of three magi. We even have three traditional names for the Magi: Gaspar, Melchior and Balthasar.

We don't know where "the east" is. Some scholars propose that it was Iran. That is based on a story of how a Parthian army from Iran invaded the Holy Land and destroyed all of the Christian Churches in the land with the exception of that in Bethlehem. The reason that they did not destroy it was that there was a fresco of this scene on the wall of the Basilica in which the three kings were dressed as Parthians. The only difficulty is that artists often picture scenes anachronistically, picturing characters dressed in clothing that is contemporary with the artist's era and not that of the original scene.

What star did the Magi see? Was it a comet? Haley's comet did pass through around 12 B.C., but that was too early for it is believed that Jesus was born around 6 B.C. (The monk who invented the modern calendar, Dennis the Short, miscalculated the date of the birth of Jesus by several years. We know this because on his calendar Herod the Great dies in 4 B.C., and Herod tried to kill the child Jesus.)

The star was not a supernova either. A supernova is a dying star that explodes with a tremendous burst of light, so bright that one can see it during the day. There were no supernovas in this era. We know this because we have day-to-day astrological records from China.

What was the star of Bethlehem? It was most probably a syzygy. This is when certain planets line up in a straight line looking out from the earth. In 7 B.C., the planets Mars, Jupiter and Saturn lined up in the constellation Pisces. Jupiter was the planet that announced the birth of a king, and Saturn pointed to the land of Palestine. Finally, Pisces was the sign that pointed to the end of time. It doesn't take too much imagination to read from this that a king (Jupiter) is born for the Jews (Saturn) for the end of time (Pisces).

When the Magi arrived in Jerusalem, they went to the logical place that one would search for a newborn king: the palace. Herod inquired of the scribes where this king was supposed to have been born. The answer was that Micah had foretold His birth in Bethlehem. Like the Is 7:14 prophecy, the prophet probably originally meant one thing while the Holy Spirit intended a second layer of meaning. The prophet was probably speaking about a new king who would come from Bethlehem in his own days. Bethlehem was King David's hometown, but it was also a small town that would insure that the new king would have small town values and would not be contaminated by big city values. The Holy Spirit used this prophecy in another way: to foretell the site of where the Messiah would be born over 700 years later.

The Magi brought Jesus gold, frankincense and myrrh. In later tradition these gifts were explained as being gold, the gift one would give a king, frankincense, an incense one would burn to give honor to God, and myrrh, an ointment used to anoint dead bodies, to foretell how Jesus would save us through His death. Yet, isn't that a terribly morbid gift to give the mother of a newborn child. It is like bringing a mother a deed for a cemetery plot because her child would someday die.

The most probable reason why the magi brought these three gifts was that they had to travel hundreds of miles over dangerous territory. They wanted to bring gifts, but they had to bring things that were small and valuable and easily hidden. These three gifts meet those requirements, and they could have easily been sold by the Holy Family to provide for their sustenance. It was only later that these three gifts were given their symbolic meanings.

Herod ordered the death of all newborn babies in the area around Bethlehem. There were probably not all that many children in this region for this was a poor, rural area (although this was little consolation to the parents of those children who were killed). There is no outside documentation concerning the massacre of the Holy Innocents. Wouldn't Herod have issued an edict to order this killing? Probably not, for this would have been considered to be a minor affair. Herod killed over 50,000 people during his reign, including a wife, three children, and a brother-in-law who was the high priest.

Why did the Holy Family go to Egypt? Because there were many Jews living in Egypt at this time, probably more than those living in Israel. There would have been family and friends there to help them. This story also presents one of the most important themes in Matthew: that Jesus is the new Moses. The old Moses was endangered by an evil king (Pharaoh) in Egypt, the new Moses, Jesus, was endangered by an evil king (Herod) and had to flee to Egypt.

When Herod died, and it was time to go home, the Holy Family almost went to Bethlehem but it was too dangerous to go back there because Herod's son, Archelaus, had taken over Judea and he was more dangerous than his father. This is confirmed by the fact that in 6 A.D. a delegation of Jews traveled to Rome to beg Augustus to remove him as their ruler and replace him with a Roman governor, something they would never have done if Archelaus were in any way acceptable.

As we can see, most of the details of the story of Jesus' birth in Matthew are highly credible given what we know from outside sources. While this doesn't absolutely prove anything, it does lay the burden of proof on those who would deny the historicity of Matthew's account of the birth of Jesus.

Questions

1. What is the importance of the mention of Abraham's and David's names? What is the significance of the triple mention of 14 generations?
2. Why are women mentioned in Matthew's genealogy?
3. How is Matthew's account of the birth of Jesus different from Luke's?
4. Who were the Magi? What is a syzygy?

Prayer

God of the ages, You prepared for the birth of Your Son in a truly miraculous way, calling people and even the stars of heaven to give witness to the fulfillment of Your promises. Help us to see the signs of Your presence in our own times and in our own lives.

Chapter 3

The Resurrection

The Resurrection Narratives

ONE of the other major blocks of "M" material (Matthew's own source) is the Resurrection narrative found in chapter 28. Like the story of the birth of Jesus, this section also has considerable symbolic and apologetic content.

At the end of chapter 27, we hear that guards were placed outside of Jesus' tomb. Those guards were there up to the moment when Jesus rose out of the tomb. This is important, for one of the lies that Matthew was combating was that the Disciples had entered the tomb during the night and had stolen the body of Jesus. If the guards were always there, then they could not have done this. Later in chapter 28, in fact, Matthew informs us that the guards were paid a bribe to lie about this. Interestingly, this is the only Gospel in which someone actually witnesses the Resurrection. In the other accounts, the women arrive at the tomb after Jesus had already risen from the dead. It was important that the guards actually witnessed Jesus' rising so that no one could claim that there was a window of opportunity for the Disciples to perpetrate a fraud on the world.

In Matthew's account, the women go to the tomb just before dawn as they do in the other Gospels. Here, though, there are two women. (There was one in John, three in Mark and several in Luke.) The reason for two women is that one needs two to give witness to anything in the Old Testament. But remember that this is a very Jewish Gospel. Women couldn't even give witness to anything in the Old Testament. Even the Gospel of Matthew de-emphasizes the role of women. Yet, here we see two women giving witness to the Resurrection. It seems as if Matthew is saying that with the Resurrection, the rules are changed. Women are credible witnesses.

We hear about an earthquake at the moment of the Resurrection. The very pillars of the earth were shaken by these momentous events (even as they had been at the birth of Jesus). There was a blast of light. Both earthquakes and light were signs of a theophany in the Old Testament, those moments when God appeared to His people.

The angel in the tomb and then Jesus Himself tell the disciples to go to Galilee where they would meet Him. In Mark and Matthew, Jesus meets the disciples in Galilee. In Luke and John, He meets them in Jerusalem.

The Mandate

THE last verses of the Gospel are a highly theological mandate that the risen Jesus gives to His Disciples. He gives them His authority and sends them out into the world to preach the Good News. If one examines these words carefully, one sees most of the major theses that recur throughout the Gospels, e.g. that Jesus gave the Disciples authority, that He sent them out to preach, that they were to go to every nation, that they were to baptize people, etc. Typical of rabbinic teaching, these themes are repeated over and over again. There is an old saying, "If you throw enough mud at the barn door, some of it will stick."

Jesus gives this mandate on a mountain. In Matthew, mountains are important for they are places where God reveals His will.

Questions

1. Why does Matthew have to present his Resurrection account as an apology?
2. What is the significance of the mandate to the Apostles? Did it happen this way?

Prayer

Lord Jesus, we base our faith upon Your death and Resurrection. Give us the faith that we need to give witness to these mysteries in our hearts and in our actions.

Chapter 4

The Sermon on the Mount

THIS is part of the reason why Matthew has Jesus give His most important teaching on a mountain: the Sermon on the Mount (chapters 5 through 7). This is a compilation of material taken from Mark, from Q and from M. The most significant aspect of this material is that it has been grouped together by Matthew. Matthew, in fact, joins together large sections of Jesus' teachings to form five major sections of teaching: chapters 5-7; 10; 13; 18 and 23-25. It is no accident that there were five sections, for that is the number of books in the Hebrew Torah (the Pentateuch). These five sections of teaching are the new Torah for the new Israel.

The Beatitudes

WHILE the old Ten Commandments were very clear do's and don'ts, the new commandments, the Beatitudes, are invitations to generosity. This is a typical Jewish way of teaching. One presents the goal, even though one knows full well that people can't reach that goal any time soon. It is similar to an idea about sin and conversion found in the Old Testament. Sin is missing the mark (like an arrow shot at a target that misses the bull's-eye). Conversion is not hitting the bull's-eye, it is getting closer to the bull's-eye. Conversion tends to come in degrees, as is seeking virtue. One could try to live the Beatitudes all of one's life and never get it perfect, but that is OK as long as one keeps trying.

These sayings are called the Beatitudes (in Greek, the *Makarioi*). This word could be translated as either "blessed" or "happy." These are wisdom teachings: ways to live the good life.

There are two versions of the Beatitudes in the Gospels: one found in Mt 5:3-12 and the other found in Lk 6:20-26. Since the Beatitudes appear in Matthew and Luke but do not appear in Mark, then it means that they come from Q (which we suggested might have been collected by Matthew the Apostle). There are quite a few differences between the two accounts. Which version is the closest to what Jesus actually proclaimed?

Matthew has eight blessed statements while Luke has four blessed statements and four curses. The mixture of blessings and curses is a more Jewish way of stating things. Remember how Joshua renewed the covenant by having priests stand on two opposing mountains. Those on one mountain proclaimed, "Blessed are those who keep the commandments," while those on the other side proclaimed, "Cursed are those who do not keep the commandments." Because Luke's version with the four blessings and curses is more Jewish, we can conclude that it is probably closer to what Jesus actually proclaimed. (This is not the only time that Luke is more original than Matthew, i.e., when Jesus says in Luke that one must hate one's parents to follow Him.)

The Beatitudes in Matthew also differ from those in Luke because they are more spiritualized than those found in Luke. While Matthew speaks of the "poor in spirit," Luke speaks of the "poor." Matthew speaks of those who "hunger and thirst for justice" while Luke speaks of those who "hunger and thirst."

When one reads Matthew's version of the Beatitudes, it is good to keep in mind the community for which he was writing. It was a group of Jewish Christians who were being persecuted by the Pharisees/rabbis. It is not that Matthew is making this material up, but the way he states things is shaped by his community's needs.

The first Beatitude is a good example: "Blessed are the poor in spirit." One would think that it would be better to be rich in spirit, a very spiritual person. But Matthew is contrasting the members of his community who were broken and humble from the Pharisees who were proud and arrogant. They thought that they were "rich in spirit." Today we might say that they were full of themselves. It is therefore more blessed to be like the humble Christians than the powerful Jewish leaders.

It is easy to identify those who hunger and thirst for righteousness as the Christians, but remember that their righteousness is not found in the strict observance of the law. It is to be found in the practice of mercy, such as we saw in the way that Joseph treated Mary when she was pregnant.

"Blessed are the meek." Again, it is easy to identify Matthew's community as meek. They had no real power. They couldn't expel anyone from the synagogue. Yet, they are promised that they would inherit the land. This makes no sense if one is thinking at a logical level. It is said that "might makes right." Yet, the Gospel points to a different way of seeing things: God's way. Power and guilt and fear do not bring conversion, they only bring conformity. Only love can bring people to conversion.

"Blessed are the pure (clean) of heart for they shall see God." The heart in the Bible is where one thinks, one feels with one's guts. If one is pure of heart, then one is always thinking about one thing, one is single minded. If one is always thinking about God, then one is bound to see signs of God's presence wherever one looks.

The community is counseled to be merciful. In times of persecution, it is so easy to be angry and resentful. It is easy to become that which one hates most. Mercy reminds one that the "enemy" is really a broken person who needs one's forgiveness and love.

The Beatitudes close with a warning about persecution. Christians in Matthew's community are told that they are actually in good company for even the prophets suffered in Old Testament times. Thus, far from being a sign of their exclusion from Israel, their persecution was actually part of a long-standing tradition in Israel.

This question of persecution and suffering was always a difficult concept in New Testament times. One would think that if one were faithful to Jesus, then everything would work out in one's life. Yet, the exact opposite often happened. It seemed as if the more faithful one was, the greater the price one had to pay. New Testament authors tried to show that this was all part of God's plan. It was not an accident or a question of being in the wrong place at the wrong time. In their suffering for Christ, the members of the community were one with Christ Who had suffered for us.

The Law

AFTER recounting a couple of wisdom sayings, Jesus addresses the question of whether the law of Israel was still valid or not. The Pharisees/rabbis had accused Matthew and his community of rejecting the tradition of Israel. This section shows that this is not the case. Like the Pharisees/rabbis, Matthew's community was committed to keeping the smallest regulation of the law. Matthew's community was therefore a very traditional Jewish Christian community.

Matthew's attitude toward the law contrasts with Paul's. While in Matthew we hear that the law is always valid and Christians should respect it, in Paul's writings (which predate this Gospel by a couple of decades) we hear that Christians are free from the observance of the law. In our present day Christianity, while we do have elements of our faith that come from Judaism (e.g., the Ten Commandments, the celebration of the Eucharist which is based on Jewish liturgy, etc.), for the most part we do not observe Jewish law. Why is it that we tend to follow Paul's view on this matter rather than Matthew's? The answer is demographics. In the very early days of the Church, most converts were Jewish. As time went by, however, and especially after the decrees of Jamnia, the balance shifted dramatically. Most of the new converts were now Gentiles who were much more influenced by Paul's writings than Matthew's.

Building a Fence Around the Law

AS we have already seen, the Pharisaic attitude toward the law was to treat it with tremendous respect and follow it rigorously. They attempted to keep all 613 commandments in the Old Testament. They produced interpretations as to what the laws meant, the process of loosing and binding. There was, for example, a commandment that one was not to eat a kid goat boiled in its mother's milk. The reason for this law seems to be that this was a form of worship to the pagan fertility gods (for both the baby goat and the mother's milk were signs of fertility). The rabbis at the time of Jesus did not understand this, though, and so they had to find an interpretation for this particular law.

They eventually decided that it meant that one was not supposed to eat meat and dairy products at the same time (a major part of the Jewish dietary law).

Having arrived at this interpretation, they then built a fence around the law. How could one be sure that one never broke even the smallest part of this law? This was why observant Jews had two sets of pots and pans, two sets of dishes and silverware, two sinks, two refrigerators, etc. in order to create a kosher kitchen.

Jesus rejected the legalistic interpretations of this technique, even if He did accept the idea of building a fence around the law. The only difference was that He did it in a more spiritual manner. He reinterpreted the Commandments to apply them in a wider manner. In the Old Testament it says, "Thou shall not kill." Jesus said that it was not enough to refuse to actually kill someone, for one would also kill a brother if one hated or insulted that person. One could kill a person's reputation or one's hopes. One could commit slow motion suicide by not taking care of one's health. One could quietly accede to killing by not fighting for the rights of the unborn or of war victims.

Likewise, adultery is committed not only when one sleeps with a married person. It also occurs in one's dirty thoughts about another. Here we have to be a bit cautious, however, for we often have thoughts that pop into our minds. For something to be a sin, we have to make a choice to do what is wrong. Thus, the initial thought is not a sin if we didn't choose to have it. It is a sin when we choose to keep thinking about it or act on it.

Jesus also changes the Old Testament law concerning divorce. Divorce was permitted in the Old Testament, but Jesus rejects that custom (here and again in Mt 19). This prohibition is also found in Mark, Luke and First Corinthians. There is absolutely no question that these are Jesus' words (and not just ideas made up by the Church as some people would argue).

Notice, that in all of these interpretations, Jesus gives the pronouncements in His own name. Remember how Matthew presents Jesus as the new Moses, but here we see Jesus as much greater than Moses. The first Moses could not give Israel a law upon his own authority. He could only hand on a law which God had given him. Jesus, the second Moses, has the authority of God Himself so He could proclaim this new law in His own name.

Jesus continues His reinterpretation of the law when He speaks about taking oaths. The Hebrew formula for taking an oath was, "As the Lord lives," or "As long as the heavens are above us." Jesus said that we should not be using God and the heavens and Jerusalem to prove anything. It is manipulative, using these holy things just to bear witness to what we are saying. We should just tell the truth instead.

Jesus then speaks about revenge and how we should deal with our enemies. In the Old Testament, the rule was "an eye for an eye and a tooth for a tooth." This was actually a rule that limited the extent to which people would seek revenge. One would no longer kill those who had harmed one. But Jesus takes this to a new level. We should not seek revenge. We should, in fact, be generous with those who oppress us, giving them more than they even asked from us.

Likewise, we should not hate our enemies. We should love them and pray for them. Only love destroys the power of hate and evil. God loves everyone, even the people who least deserve it. We are called to do the same.

Jesus finishes His instructions with the call to be perfect as God is perfect. We are being invited to be perfect in love. This is our goal, but it will take us the rest of our lives to reach that goal. This is not a call to perfectionism, only to do the best we can.

Almsgiving, Prayer and Fasting

THE next three topics addressed by Jesus need to be understood within a certain context. When the temple in Jerusalem was destroyed, people went up to the rabbis and asked them how they could now obtain forgiveness for their sins. Before the temple had been destroyed, they only had to offer a sacrifice. The rabbis answered these people that they could now give alms, pray and fast. These are the exact things that Jesus commanded His followers to do, but He tells them not to do them in the same way that the Pharisees did. They were to do them for the right reasons and with the proper motives.

When one gives alms, one is to do it in a manner that does not draw attention to oneself. But isn't this the exact opposite of what He said when He told His disciples to let their light be seen by all. We have these two seemingly contradictory ideas because this is a very Jewish way of speaking, giving one extreme and the other. The truth lies somewhere in the middle. This is why it is so dangerous to quote scripture out of context. If one only quotes one side of an issue, then one might be missing the other side that balances out the first saying.

In giving alms, we have to ask ourselves why we are doing it. Is it to bring attention to ourselves or to help others? Do we do it in such a way that we seek not to humiliate the person receiving our assistance? Do we at times need to publicize what we are doing in order to motivate others to help? Are our motives sometimes a bit mixed and how can we be honest with ourselves about what our true motives are?

We should apply these same ideas when we pray. We are not praying to be seen. We are praying to offer God praise. The pagans would pray to their gods by endlessly repeating exact formulas. There was no question of interior disposition as long as one was precise in the formula. Christians were not to pray in that manner. Jesus, in fact, offers them an example of how they should pray. He teaches His listeners the Our Father.

There are two versions of the Our Father: one here in Matthew and one in Luke. Matthew's version is a fully developed prayer while Luke's version is a series of disjointed petitions. Once again, Luke is probably more original, recording what Jesus actually said while Matthew gives us the prayer that was being used by the community when Matthew was writing his Gospel (80-85 A.D.).

The third topic in this section is fasting. In Jesus' days, when someone died one would perform ritual actions like tearing one's clothes, putting dust on one's head, etc. This was also done when one fasted. Fasting thus became a ritual for mourning for one's sins.

Why do we fast? There are a number of reasons. It helps put food in its proper perspective in our lives because we often misuse food. It reminds us that Christ is more important than food.

By making this choice we are healing some of the wounds that we bring into our lives by sinning (for now we have replaced the wrong choice with the proper choice). Fasting also teaches us discipline, helping us to say "no" to temptation and "yes" to Christ. It also places us in solidarity with those who do not have enough to eat. We are sharing in their hunger, and thus destroying their feelings of alienation and abandonment.

After a series of other wisdom teachings on how we should depend upon the providence of God, how we should not judge others, etc., we are told that we must make a choice as to what we will build upon. If we build upon sand, then what we build will not survive the coming storm. If we build upon rock (Jesus), then what we build will endure.

Questions

1. Why does Matthew place these teachings upon a mountain?
2. What is the difference between the Beatitudes and the Ten Commandments? Between Matthew's Beatitudes and Luke's?
3. Why do we as Christians not observe all of the Jewish law?
4. Are we called to build a fence around the law today?
5. What is the significance of fasting? How should we fast? Give alms? Pray?

Prayer

Lord God, let me be filled with such a generosity of spirit that I do not even want to count the cost. Let me always remember the goal toward which I am directing my life: Jesus, Your Son.

Chapter 5

The Structure of the Gospel

HAVING looked at the Sermon on the Mount, an extended section of Jesus' teachings, we can now speak a little more about the structure Matthew gave to his Gospel. Unlike Mark who pasted together his Gospel as best he could, Matthew was meticulous in developing a very clear structure to his Gospel. This was part of his rabbinic background: he was as meticulous in shaping his message as rabbis were in interpreting the law.

We have already seen that Matthew gathered Jesus' teachings into five major sections of discourse. This was a type of new Torah for the new Israel (for the old Torah, the Pentateuch, was the normative series of books for the old Israel). On either side of these discourse sections, there are sections of narrative that tell what Jesus did. Thus, there is a narrative section, then a discourse, then a narrative, then a discourse, etc.

These sections are not arranged at random. The first section prepares for the second, the second for the third, etc. We saw how the first section of narrative presented Jesus as the new Moses. The old Moses was threatened by an evil king in Egypt, the new Moses had to flee to Egypt to escape from the threats of an evil king. The old Moses fasted for forty days on a mountain, and the new Moses fasted for forty days in the desert. This prepares for the second section, which is a discourse section: the Sermon on the Mount. The first section showed us that Jesus is the new Moses, so when He reveals the new law for the new Israel, He does it on a mountain (just like the first Moses who received the law for the old Israel on Mount Sinai). Then, in the third section, Jesus performs a series of miracles to affirm that He had the authority to give commandments. What would the perfect number of miraculous deeds be to demonstrate His authority? The answer is ten, just like there were Ten Commandments. One of the names for the Ten Commandments, in fact, is the Decalogue. That name means the "ten words," but it could also be translated as the "ten deeds." Thus, the "ten deeds" showed that Jesus could proclaim the "ten words," His new law for the new Israel.

This sort of structure, one section preparing for the next, is called a staircase pattern. With this type of structure, the climax is at the end: the death and Resurrection of Jesus.

Yet, there is also another structure in the Gospel. This is called a chiasm. With chiasms, there are an odd number of sections in a piece of literature. The first and the last sections have similarities, the second and the second last, the third and the third last, etc. The central section is the most important part of the chiasm. In the Gospel of Matthew, the central section is chapter 13, the instructions Jesus gives on the kingdom of heaven.

The chapter begins with the parable of the seed that falls on the path, among the rocks, among the weeds, and finally on good soil. This parable is Jesus' way of explaining how one should love the Lord with one's whole heart (intellect), soul (willing to risk one's life in times of persecution) and strength (one's possessions).

Like the Gospel of Mark, we hear that people will hear these things but refuse to believe. Jesus will preach the parables to hold people responsible. Jesus also speaks of the Disciples' good fortune for they were given the gift of being able to hear and see the promises of the Old Testament fulfilled.

The parable of the weeds among the wheat is typical of the Gospel of Matthew, which often speaks of the coming judgment. In this case, the question is why does God wait to punish the evil and reward the just. The answer is that God is waiting so that everyone had an opportunity to change their ways. If God were to send His wrath too soon, then some of the good might suffer along with the evil.

There are then two parables that deal with the gradual growth of the kingdom. Why did the kingdom not dawn quickly and powerfully? We still ask the same question, "Why, after two thousand years, has goodness not yet conquered evil?"

The answer is that it has dawned, but in small ways. Every time that someone forgives another, or trusts in God in the midst of suffering, or chooses to help a person in need, etc., the kingdom is dawning. Today we might speak of the butterfly effect: one small action causes a change in something else that triggers another change which in turn triggers still another change, etc. This is the meaning of the parable of the mustard seed (that things begin in small ways) and that of the yeast (that these small changes can change the world).

The importance of the kingdom in our lives is seen in the parable of the buried treasure and the pearl of great price. One might have to make sacrifices to obtain what is really important. The kingdom requires such sacrifices. Matthew's community knew this lesson. They had been asked to sacrifice their places of worship, their families, their way of earning a living, etc. in order to be Christians. As was said before, we will all have to pay a price and face a certain amount of persecution. But even if we are not being persecuted, we will still have to say "no" to certain things in order to be able to say "yes" to others. Paul speaks of being crucified to the world so that he might live in Christ.

There is then another judgment parable when Matthew speaks of the kingdom being like a net thrown in the water. One catches everything in the net, and fishermen must sort out the good from the bad. This is what will happen at the end of time, those who are good will be separated from those who are evil.

In spite of all of this wisdom, Jesus was rejected in His hometown. Interestingly, in Mark Jesus was rejected after Jesus performed different types of miracles. Here the emphasis is on instruction into the ways of God. This is something that one would expect from a rabbi like the author of this Gospel.

Question

1. Why did Matthew create such an elaborate series of structures for his Gospel?

Prayer

Teach me to order my life, O Lord, through the spiritual disciplines that help me to make sense of Who You are and who I am and what You want for me.

Chapter 6

How Matthew Is Different

The Role of Peter

IN chapter 13, we hear of the establishment of the kingdom of heaven. This is a discourse section. What follows is a narrative section that runs from chapter 14 to 17. The theme of the narrative section is how Jesus passes on the authority of the Disciples and especially to Peter.

In Matthew 16:13ff, Jesus asks His disciples at Caesarea Philippi who people said that He was. Peter responds that He is the Messiah, the Son of the Living God. This is similar to what we find in Mark (with the addition of the words "the Son of the Living God"). In Mark, though, Jesus predicts His Passion and death and Peter is horrified for he wanted Jesus to be a powerful Messiah. Peter tells Jesus not to say those things, and Jesus responds, "Get behind Me Satan." Matthew has these same ideas 16:21ff, but in between Peter's profession of faith and Jesus' strong words to Peter, there is a commissioning that does not appear in Mark.

Jesus tells Peter that His words do not come from a human source, but rather have been revealed by God. Jesus gives Peter a new name (he was Simon before this), a name that means "rock." Peter was to be the firm foundation upon which He was going to build His Church. (Remember the house built on rock and not sand.) This is the only place in all four Gospels where we hear Jesus use the word "Church."

Jesus tells Peter that the gates of the nether world would not prevail against the Church. Jesus was proclaiming this at Caesarea Philippi where the water of the Jordan comes bubbling out of the earth. Just above these waters there is a cave in which there had been worship of the pagan gods from time immemorial. It was known as the gates of death or the underworld. In Jesus' mind, it represented the forces of evil that would oppose His Church but which would never conquer it.

Jesus presents Peter with the keys of the kingdom. In the Old Testament, only God had the keys. They were the keys to life, to death, and to rain. In the New Testament, it was Jesus Who had this authority, and now He was handing it on to Peter.

Jesus gives Peter the power to loose and to bind. As we have seen, this was the power that the rabbis possessed, to be able to decide what the rules of living the faith were to be.

Some people question whether the authority being given to Peter was given to him alone. Wasn't it given to all of the Disciples? There is, after all, a statement in Mt 18:18 which seems to imply that. Was Peter the only one receiving the authority or was it all of the Disciples?

When we examine this section of narrative (that which runs from chapter 14 to 17), we notice that Matthew has placed a number of passages about Peter in these chapters. He wanted him to be the center of attention.

The first passage is when Jesus walks on the water (14:22ff). In the other Gospels, only Jesus walks on the water. In Matthew, Peter joins Jesus walking. He gets out of the boat and walks on the water. Admittedly, Peter does not make it all that far before his faith falters, but he does get out of the boat and try to trust.

In the next chapter, the reference to Peter is a bit more subtle. In 15:15, Peter asks Jesus to explain one of His parables. In Mark, it was an unnamed disciple who asked this question. Here it is Peter. This change is not all that important except when it is viewed in light of the various passages in these chapters in which Peter's role is emphasized.

In chapter 16, we have Peter's profession of faith and his reception of the keys of the kingdom. The keys of the kingdom section, as we shall see, is not found in the other Gospels.

In 17:1ff, Peter is one of the Disciples who witnesses the Transfiguration. This story is found in the other Gospels. One of Matthew's techniques is to use some of the stories found in the other Gospels and then add others that appear only in his Gospel.

Then, at the end of chapter 17, verses 24ff, Jesus tells Peter to go fishing so that he might catch a fish with a coin in its mouth with which he could pay the temple tax for himself and Jesus.

Thus, it is clear that Peter is the central character of these chapters. Even if the other Disciples receive a share in Jesus' authority, it is Peter who receives the call to be Christ's vicar. Furthermore, this Gospel was written around 80-85 A.D. Peter died sometime around 67 A.D. Matthew was thus not speaking only about Peter, he was speaking about the role that Peter played in the community (what we, today, would call the papacy).

But did Jesus really say these things? What do the other Gospels say about all of this?

The first Gospel written was probably that written by Mark. In that Gospel, the disciples are not seen to be models of faith. They are confused and they only come to understand Jesus' message at the cross. There is no scene in which Peter receives the keys of the kingdom. Yet, even in this Gospel, Peter is always the first among the Apostles whenever their names are listed, and he is always one of the three important apostles.

What does Luke say? Luke does not have a keys of the kingdom passage, but he does have another passage that is significant. It occurs at the Last Supper. Food and meals were very important for Luke. Many of the parables speak of meals. Even heaven is pictured as a heavenly banquet. Thus, it should not surprise us that some of Jesus' most important instructions in this Gospel occur at the Last Supper. Add to this the idea found in ancient literature that one's final testament was considered to be one's most important instructions, then Jesus' words to His Disciples at the Last Supper should be considered to be His most significant instructions.

Jesus first tells the Disciples that they should not misuse their authority as the leaders of the Gentiles do. They were to serve others and not seek power and prestige.

He then turned to Peter and told him that Satan had decided to sift them like wheat, but that he (Peter) would be called to strengthen his brothers when he turned back.

Like Matthew's keys of the kingdom passage, we hear that Satan would oppose the Church. Furthermore, Peter was to have a significant role in the Church by strengthening it. The other part of the passage refers to Peter's turning back, an obvious reference to Peter's triple denial and his need to turn back from that.

What about John's Gospel? The Gospel of John is the most anti-authority of the Gospels. The word "apostle" never once appears in the Gospel. Everyone is a disciple, a follower. No one is in charge other than Jesus and no one acts as an envoy (which is the meaning of the word "apostle"). There is no list of the twelve Apostles anywhere in the Gospel. Furthermore, when the Apostles do appear, they often are portrayed as bumbling characters and not as heroes.

Yet, in John 21, we do have a passage in which Peter received authority over the others. Jesus asks Peter three times, "Do you love me?" Jesus does this because Peter had denied Jesus three times. This was an opportunity for Peter to heal the triple denial. (This idea was found in Luke when Peter was told to "turn back.") It was also a way to tie the authority that Peter was receiving with the call to love.

What authority did Peter receive? He was called to lead the flock, to be its shepherd. Jesus presented Himself as the Good Shepherd in this Gospel. Peter was now being given that authority.

Within that context, one can also understand the triple "do you love me?" It is a reminder to Peter that even though he is the shepherd, he was as flawed as the rest of us. He should remember that he was a sinner so that he not become pompous. This is very similar to a ritual performed during the old rite of the coronation of the popes. A Capuchin Franciscan would follow the new pope around and he would light a clump of dried flax (the raw material of linen) three times. It would go up like flash powder. Each time he lit the flax, he would whisper into the ear of the pope, *"sic transit gloria mundi,"* which means, "So passes the glory of the world." In modern English, we might say, "Don't get uppity, you're going to die some day."

Even the Gospel of John, which is prejudiced against authority, admits that someone is needed to guide the flock.

Thus, what can we say about the keys of the kingdom? While only Matthew specifically mentions keys, three of the Gospels speak of Peter being given authority. Even Mark implies this authority by listing Peter as the first of the Apostles. All four Gospels thus recognize Peter's authority at some level, and even the Gospel which one would least expect to emphasize authority, John, speaks of Peter's role as the shepherd of the Church. The Gospels might not exactly agree when Jesus said it or how He said it, but they agree that He said or did something that made Peter the leader of the Apostles.

Parables of Judgment

WE have already seen two parables that speak about the judgment at the end of time. There was the story of the weeds sown in the midst of the wheat. The owner of the field orders it not to be separated until the final harvest. There was also the net thrown into the sea that collected both good and evil. The fisherman would separate the two, saving the good and discarding the evil.

One could also speak of the parable of the unforgiving servant (18:21ff). A servant who owed his master a very great sum of money is forgiven and given more time to pay his debt. Immediately after leaving his audience with his master, the servant runs into a fellow servant who owes him only a fraction of that amount. Instead of showing him the same mercy that he had received, he has his fellow servant thrown into debtors prison until the debt should be paid in full. The lesson is that mercy will be shown to those who practice mercy.

One small detail of the story should also be clarified. The servant was thrown into prison until his debt was fully paid. Some people have said that this is a lesson about purgatory, which teaches that souls must remain there until the last part of their debt due to their sins is paid. We have to be careful here, though, for this parable was not speaking about purgatory, and it is dangerous to apply parables in a way that they were not really intended. Jesus paid the price for our sins, the entire price. We have nothing to pay in purgatory. It is not where we make up for our sins; it is where we heal the wounds that our sins have brought into our hearts. God forgives all, but we have weakened ourselves with our bad choices and find it difficult to embrace that love. Purgatory is a place of purification, not punishment. One sees this when one reads Paul's comments on it in 1 Corinthians 3.

A second judgment parable is found in 20:1: the parable of the workers in the vineyard. An owner of a vineyard goes out and hires workers at various times of the day. At the end of the day, he pays his workers the same wage, even though some of the workers had worked all day long while others had only worked for an hour or so. Those who worked all day long felt that this was unfair. The owner's response was that he was free to do whatever he wanted with his own money. He was fair to those who worked all day and generous with the others. This was his prerogative.

Couldn't God treat the newcomers, the Gentiles, with the same mercy with which He had formerly treated the Jews? Couldn't God show mercy to whomever He willed? God's ways are not like our ways. God's ways are not "fair" in the way that the world judges things. If God only judged us with justice, then we would all face eternal punishment for even the smallest infraction. We hope that God will be merciful as well as just at the last judgment.

Furthermore, if we were really filled with God's love, wouldn't we be thrilled if He showed His generosity and love to others? The measure of our true love is how joyous we would be if our worst enemy in the world were to get to heaven before us.

Then there is the parable of the two sons (21:28ff). It contrasts two sons, one who says he will obey his father and the other who says he will not. The one who says he will obey his father then decides not to do what his father wanted. The other son who said he would not do his father's will changes his mind and does it. Jesus asks who really did what the father wanted. He then tells His listeners that sinners would enter heaven long before the self-righteous.

The parable of the wedding feast offers another insight into the kingdom. Many people are invited to the kingdom, but only a few respond. So God calls people from the streets so that His banquet might be full. When God calls us, we have to be ready and willing to respond to His call and leave all to follow Him. One odd element of the parable is that one of those who arrived was dressed inappropriately and he was thrown out. No matter what our background is when we are called, we must prepare ourselves well (the significance of being dressed appropriately).

In 24:45, we hear that we should always be ready for the return of the Lord. We don't know when the end of the world will occur, but we should always be ready. Many sacristies have a sign that says, "Priest of God, say this Mass as if it were your first Mass, say it as if it were your last Mass, say it as if it were your only Mass." Wouldn't it be good if we lived every day that way, never leaving unsaid or undone anything lest we never have another chance.

The parable of the ten virgins continues this idea. Five virgins were wise and they prepared well for the delay of the groom, five were foolish and did not prepare for this. Those who were wise were welcomed into the banquet, while those who were not could not enter.

Again, we should be careful not to over interpret this parable. Some people complain that the wise virgins were selfish and should have shared their oil with the others. That is not really a part of the parable. It was proclaimed to remind people to be prepared.

The parable of the talents (25:14ff) states that we will be judged on how well we use the abilities that God gave us. We are not expected to do more than we can, but we are expected to use well those abilities. They are not our own property. They are gifts from God (cf. 1 Cor 12).

Finally, there is the parable of the sheep and the goats. In ancient times, sheep and goats appeared much more alike than they do today. It was a bit of work to separate one from the other.

The basis for judgment is how well one treated those who were in need. When one assisted them, one was really serving Christ. This reminds us of the horizontal dimension of our faith. It is not enough to love God and ignore the needs of those around us. The vertical and horizontal dimensions of our faith must be balanced.

All of these parables remind us that there is a coming judgment. Some of these parables are also found in the other Gospels while others are found only here. All together, they form a unified message concerning the future reckoning of our lives (much as the combination of sections dealing with Peter formed a unified message in chapters 14-17).

While our spiritual life should not be based upon fear, once in a while it helps us to keep things in mind. We will not live forever, and will have to face the Lord with what we have done and what we have not done.

Jesus' Attitude toward the Pharisees and Sadducees

IN all four Gospels, one can sense a certain tension between Jesus and the Pharisees and Sadducees. Jesus condemned the Pharisees for what He felt was hypocrisy. The Pharisees and the Sadducees baited Jesus to see if they could make Him say or do something that they could use against Him.

This tension becomes explosive in the Gospel of Matthew. Remember, this Gospel was written by a community that had just been kicked out of the synagogue and which faced possible martyrdom. Furthermore, if our theory about the Gospel's authorship is valid, then the Matthew who wrote the final version of this Gospel might have been a Pharisee himself (which would make his feeling of betrayal all the more acute).

We begin to see the tension early in the Gospel, in 3:7, when John the Baptist calls the Pharisees and Sadducees who came out to hear him "a brood of vipers." Snakes are a symbol for the evil one. John was thus saying that the Pharisees' and Sadducees' motivation for coming out to hear him was not a desire for conversion. He was accusing them of being Satanic.

In Matthew 15 Jesus attacks the superficiality of the "tradition of the fathers." For a number of generations, Pharisees had been interpreting the law to apply it to everyday life. Jesus attacks those interpretations, which were simply a way of getting around the obligations of the law. His most striking example was that which speaks of the commandment to honor one's parents. This was interpreted as an obligation to help them financially if they were in need. Yet, some of the rabbis allowed one to avoid this responsibility by saying that the money one intended to give one's parents was the one-tenth that one had promised to the temple. Thus, the parents didn't get anything. Jesus strongly condemned this hypocrisy.

The material contained in this chapter had already been treated in Mark's Gospel so it wasn't all that new. Remember, this is typical of Matthew. He used what the other Gospels said, and then he added his own particular material to reinforce the message. The added material is found in chapter 23 when Jesus' attack on the scribes (doctors of the law) and Pharisees becomes vicious.

He first accuses the scribes and Pharisees of not doing what they tell others to do. The scribes and Pharisees would meet every evening after a long day's work to determine the obligations of the law (the process of loosing and binding). Some of those interpretations become onerous (e.g., counting the grains of salt one used so one could give one-tenth of them to the temple).

Jesus also accuses the scribes and Pharisees of seeking the admiration of the public but not living with an interior disposition of conversion. He speaks of them widening their phylacteries. These were small boxes with leather straps attached so that they could tie them to their foreheads and arms while they were praying. There was a small scroll inside the box with a bit of the Torah, so they were wearing the law. The tassels were the threads that one did not cut off of one's undergarments. Those threads thus stuck out and were a constant reminder of one's commitment to the covenant. Loving to widen phylacteries and tassels meant that Jesus felt that the Pharisees were just putting on a show.

Jesus also speaks of how they loved honored positions in the marketplace and titles of honor. This is a danger that any public figure faces, especially the clergy. One can begin to like or even need the signs of respect that one receives.

One has to ask whether this condemnation is a fair evaluation for all the Pharisees. When one reads ancient literature, one receives a fairly positive picture of most Pharisees and rabbis. Was it only some Pharisees who were this way (just as some present-day Christians fall into the same trap)? Furthermore, were these Jesus' words or did Matthew exaggerate them? We just don't know. There are bits and pieces of this material in the other Gospels, but most of it is found only in Matthew and that makes us wonder. Unfortunately, we can't reach any conclusions concerning this material's origin.

The real danger is that these verses and others that attack the leaders of the Jews might be taken out of context and used by those who desire to rationalize some form of anti-Semitism. We have to remember, the Jewish people are people of the covenant and God is always faithful to His promises. They are still the chosen people and should be treated with respect.

Furthermore, it was not because of the Jews or the Romans that Jesus died. It was our fault. He died for our sins. He died out of love for us. It would be a horrible irony if we allowed that act of love to become the reason or excuse to hate.

Differences in the Passion Narrative

THROUGHOUT the story of the Passion of Christ, there are a number of differences between Matthew's version of the events and that which Mark reported. By examining these differences, we might get a bit of information about what Matthew considered to be most important.

In Matthew 21, Jesus enters Jerusalem on Palm Sunday. Most of the details are essentially the same as those found in Mark, but there is a small difference in how Jesus fulfills Zechariah 9:9. The prophet spoke of the Messiah entering Jerusalem on a donkey, on the colt of a donkey. The significance of this passage was that it was contrasting how the Jewish Messiah would enter Jerusalem as opposed to the generals and kings of the pagan nations and how they would enter cities that they had conquered. The Jewish Messiah would enter Jerusalem with humility.

But how many donkeys would the Messiah ride? In Mark, Luke and John, Jesus rides on one young donkey. That was the meaning of the original saying for it was written in poetry and Hebrew poetry often used parallelism to convey a point (saying the same thing twice or more often to give a fuller picture of the event or to add emphasis). By mentioning a donkey, a colt of a donkey, Zechariah was saying "one young donkey." For some reason, Matthew didn't quite get it. He speaks of two donkeys. We do not know why he interpreted the text that way, unless he was being overly literal because of his Pharisaic background.

Another difference between Matthew and the other Gospels is Matthew's treatment of Judas. We get more information in this Gospel than we do in the others concerning his betrayal (26:14ff) and his eventual suicide (27:3ff). This is the Gospel in which we hear that Judas received thirty pieces of silver. There are three possible explanations for this sum of money. It could be symbolic because this was the amount of money that one would be expected to reimburse the owner of a slave if he were gored by an ox (meaning that Jesus was worth little more than a slave to those involved in this plot). It could be a fulfillment of Zechariah 11:12 in which the Good Shepherd was paid thirty pieces of silver (but in this case it is the betrayer of the shepherd of the money who gets the money). The third possibility is that it simply was the amount of money that Judas was paid.

As in the other Gospels, Jesus predicts His betrayal at the Last Supper, indicating Judas as the one who would betray Him. Judas also betrays Jesus in the Garden of Gethsemane with a kiss. A kiss on the cheek is still used in many European and Middle Eastern cultures. Judas kissed Jesus because the garden was dark and the soldiers who came out to arrest Jesus did not know Him well. Jesus had preached in Galilee and was not well known in Jerusalem. The kiss was a way of making sure that they arrested the right person, but it was also a horribly intimate way to betray Jesus' trust.

The story of the death of Judas is material not contained in the other Gospels (although a somewhat different version of it can be found in Acts 1:17ff). Matthew and Acts agree that Judas killed himself (although they seem to differ on how he did this) and they both agreed that the money paid for the betrayal of Jesus was used to buy a field in which the poor were buried (although in Matthew it is the priests who buy the field and in Acts it is Judas himself who buys it). Matthew also emphasizes Judas' grief and guilt as well as the cold-hearted response by the priests and the elders. This is typical of Matthew, that the guilt of the leaders of the Jews was emphasized over and over again.

There is a slight difference at the Last Supper in the words of institution for the Eucharist (26:26ff). When Jesus called the cup of the blood of the covenant shed for many, Matthew includes the phrase, "for the forgiveness of sins." This ties the formula used even closer to the theology presented in the Songs of the Suffering Servant in Isaiah. This servant was a mysterious figure who meekly brought justice to all the nations through his suffering and death "for the forgiveness of sins." Jewish theologians were not sure who this person was. Jesus, here and in other places, applied the prophesy to Himself. By saying these things, He was explicitly tying the Eucharistic meal to the Cross and saying that both brought us freedom from our sins.

The trial before the high priests is not all that different from that contained in the other Gospels, but that before Pilate has a couple of significant changes. All of the changes are intended to lessen the guilt of the Romans and to place the blame entirely upon the leaders of the Jews. Pilate wants to let Jesus go free, and Pilate's wife lets him know that she had a dream that warned her and Pilate not to harm Jesus. The leaders of the Jews, however, insist upon Jesus' death. Pilate washes his hands as a sign that he was not responsible for the death of Jesus (he was washing himself free of responsibility for what was happening). The leaders of the Jews respond to this symbolic action by saying that Jesus' blood should be upon them and their children. Throughout history these verses have often been used by those who wished to persecute the Jewish people. One cannot emphasize enough how these lines must be read within their context. Furthermore, if the blood of Jesus is upon anyone, it is actually upon us because of our sins.

As in the other Gospels, when Jesus is condemned to death, He is mocked and tortured by the soldiers. In Matthew's Gospel, instead of putting a purple robe on Jesus as they did in Mark and John, the soldiers put a scarlet robe upon Him in Matthew. The scarlet robe actually makes more sense than the purple robe. Purple cloth was very expensive in ancient times. It was worn by kings. How could the soldiers have had a purple robe? Scarlet, on the other hand, was worn by centurions, so it would have been easy for them to obtain a scarlet robe. The only problem is that Mark and John agree on this particular detail, and they don't agree on all that much in their accounts. No matter how difficult it is for us to understand how they obtained a purple robe, that was probably what they had.

There are a couple of small details in the account of the crucifixion that are worth mentioning. In 27:34, we hear that they offered Jesus wine mixed with gall. In Mark, it was wine mixed with myrrh. Ancient wine was more concentrated than our modern wines. It would be mixed with various ointments and perfumes. This is why it would have been mixed with myrrh, for flavoring. Gall, on the other hand, is quite a different matter. Gall is made from wormwood, and it is a hallucinogen. (There is even a narcotic drink named absinthe today). The wine mixed with gall would have been given to prisoners to deaden their pain. Even though this sounds like an act of mercy, that was not necessarily the case. Since people died of suffocation on the cross when one could no longer lift oneself up with one's legs to catch a breath, the gall might have been intended to deaden the pain a bit so that the prisoner would last longer before he died of suffocation. There are cases in which people on the cross survived for over a week before they finally succumbed.

A second small change is in the quotation "My God, My God, why have You forsaken Me." This is the first line of Psalm 22, a lamentation that expresses Jesus' feeling of abandonment. Yet, like all other lamentations, Psalm 22 ends with a profession of faith in God's deliverance. Jesus was expressing both His confusion and His trust. In Mark, Jesus says this verse in Aramaic (Eloi), while in Matthew He says it in Hebrew (Eli). Matthew might have made this change to explain why the crowd thought that Jesus was calling upon Elijah, for the Hebrew version sounds a bit more like that name.

There is a major difference in the account concerning what happens when Jesus died. In Matthew we hear that there was an earthquake and the dead rose from their graves. The earthquake was a sign that the very pillars of the earth were shaken by the death of the author of life.

In the Old Testament, the dead would rise from their graves as a signal that the kingdom of heaven was dawning. This is, in fact, why early Christians believed that the end of the world was at hand, because Jesus had risen from the dead. Therefore, the dead rising from their graves when Jesus died would be a sign that the end times had dawned.

The difficulty in arguing that this detail in the story is historic and not symbolic is the fact that if people had risen from the dead on Good Friday, then certainly someone else would have noticed it and written about it. Yet, the other Gospels ignore this fact. It must be a symbolic way of saying that the death and Resurrection of Jesus had changed the world so much that time as we know it has come to an end.

Other Differences in Matthew

IN addition to the differences we saw in the Passion Narrative, we can also speak of some other differences in the rest of the Gospel. Again, these differences can give us a good indication of what Matthew's particular point of view was.

In the account of the temptation in the desert, Matthew and Luke both speak of three temptations (Mark does not mention them.) The last temptation in Matthew is when Satan takes Jesus up on a high mountain and offers Him all of the kingdoms of the earth. Mountains were very important to Matthew, as we have already seen (e.g., the Sermon on the Mount, the Transfiguration, the mandate to the Apostles after the Resurrection, etc.). Thus, the climax of the temptation was on top of a mountain. (Luke's third temptation was in Jerusalem, a city that was very important to him.)

Another difference occurs when Jesus is asked to allow James and John to sit on His right and His left when He comes into the kingdom (21:20ff). In Mark's Gospel, it is James and John who make the request during one of three predictions of the Passion. In Matthew's Gospel, it is James' and John's mother who asks for this favor. This relieves the Apostles of the responsibility for asking for this favor. Matthew tends to treat the Apostles with more respect than the other Gospels.

Then in 18:15ff, Jesus gives instructions on how one should correct a brother who was in error. One should first confront the brother in person. This is still a very valid step for many people deal with problems by talking behind the person's back and never dealing with the problem in an adult manner.

Jesus then recommends bringing two or three witnesses with oneself when one deals with the offending brother. Again, this is a great idea for one often needs people with an independent perspective to help determine what was really said or done. People often seek out a marriage counselor or mediator to make sense of things (although it is a good idea to remember that that independent person might very well tell you that the other person is not totally at fault and that you have some things you should look at as well.)

Finally, one can bring the situation before the whole community. If the person will not listen to the entire community, then that person might have to be excommunicated. This is never a pleasant step, but the person's continued presence could be terribly destructive, creating a poisonous atmosphere. There is a time when one has to admit that the situation is destructive and it has to be dealt with (and not to ignore it to preserve a false peace). Truth and integrity are values that have to be balanced with peace and concord.

One other difference in Matthew's Gospel is the question of divorce. Mark, Luke and First Corinthians all speak of divorce once. In Matthew's Gospel, it is mentioned twice: 5:31ff and 19:aff. Remember how rabbis would say things more than once in order to make sure that their students heard what they were saying. This is probably a rabbinic technique to emphasize the importance of the teaching.

What is unusual about Matthew's version of this prohibition is that Matthew seems to have one exception: in the case of "porneia." This Greek word is the root word of "pornography." It is sometimes translated as "adultery." This is probably not what Matthew intended. Scholars believe that he was speaking about marrying someone who is too close of a blood relation. Pagans who were married to a very close relative sometimes converted and they were told to end their marriages. Remember when Paul addressed this question in First Corinthians 5:1ff when he spoke about a man who was living with his father's wife (probably his step-mother). Paul was horrified at the poor example this was giving and he recommended to the community that he be excommunicated until the man changed his ways.

Questions

1. What is the significance of the keys of the kingdom? Did Peter really receive a special share in Jesus' authority?
2. Why is it good to remember that we will be judged at the end of time?
3. Did Jesus really hate the Pharisees and Sadducees? How much of the rejection found in this Gospel comes from Jesus and how much is Matthew's?
4. How does Matthew's account of the Passion differ from that found in the other Gospels?
5. How can we see Matthew's specific point of view in the way he shapes his account?

Prayer

God, we each see things a little differently. Help me to remember that different is not always bad, sometimes it is just different. Help me to learn to accept others' differences, even if I cannot always approve of what they are doing.

Conclusion

The Value of Matthew's Gospel

EACH Gospel is the story of the ministry and teaching and life of Jesus, but each one also has its own particular value. Matthew teaches about the importance of tradition, especially the Jewish tradition that was the foundation of our faith. Every time that we celebrate the Eucharist, every time that we celebrate the new Passover of Easter, every time that we read the law and the prophets, we are participating in a heritage that goes back thousands of years.

The highly organized nature of the Gospel reminds us of the need for organization and discipline in our spiritual life. Growth in the spiritual life requires effort: prayer, fasting, obedience, humility, etc.

Matthew also teaches us about the meaning of true righteousness. It is not a question of keeping all the rules to the letter of the law. True righteousness is what Joseph exhibited when he ended up being more merciful to Mary than he thought would have been possible.

Matthew also offers us an example of the good scribe who is able to use the old and the new. Our faith is always changing, always the same. Not all new things are good, nor are all new things bad. The same is true of what is old. We have to seek what is true and good and use it to serve God's kingdom.

Finally, Matthew showed a love for the Church and its hierarchy (which in the early days was certainly not fully developed, but which, in the person of Peter, was already leading the people of God). The same Spirit Who called Peter to be the rock upon which the Church was built continues to guide our Holy Father today. The forces of the underworld will not prevail against it.

Prayer

St. Matthew, pray for us.

Part II

The Gospel of Mark

PAX
TIBI
MAR
CE

EVAN
GELIS
TA
MEVS

Chapter 1
Mark's Gospel

SOMETIME around 70 A.D. something significant happened to the Christian community. This was about 40 years after Jesus had suffered, died and rose again. The Good News had reached the "ends of the earth" of the Roman Empire. Saints Peter and Paul, in fact, had preached in Rome, the political center of that empire. They had been arrested and eventually martyred for the faith: Peter by being crucified and Paul by being decapitated. The Jewish temple in Jerusalem had just been destroyed by the Roman legions which were crushing a Jewish rebellion. The Roman Empire itself had just survived a rather traumatic period of civil war in which three individuals each claimed the throne within a period of 18 months. All of these events were already memorable.

But for the Christian community, there was an even more important thing happening: Jesus was not returning in glory. In Old Testament times, a sign of the end times was that the dead would rise from their graves. When Jesus rose from the dead on Easter Sunday, many people believed that it marked the beginning of the end of the world. Early Christians thought that some time soon Jesus was going to return in glory. We hear this in First Corinthians when some members of the community ask Paul whether they should get married. He answers that it was not really wrong to marry, but it would be better if they didn't and rather dedicated themselves to the service of the Lord while they awaited His return (which he seems to have expected anytime now). One has to wonder what the Corinthians thought when Jesus did not return.

It was around 70 A.D. that the Christians faced a turning point. They stopped speaking about how Jesus was returning right away. They began to use another expression: that He would return like a thief in the night. This meant that we didn't know exactly when He would return, but we should always be ready for it.

It was this that caused Christians to realize that there might be a future. The world was not going to end anytime soon, so

Christians had to prepare for future generations. They had to make sure that the story of Jesus would not be lost. Those who had witnessed Jesus' life and ministry were passing from the scene (some through martyrdom, others through natural death). The oral testimony had been passed down for so long now that some of the details were in danger of becoming fuzzy. Someone had to write it down in black and white.

The Holy Spirit used this realization as an opportunity to call a disciple of St. Peter, a Jewish Christian named John Mark, to write a Gospel. The Spirit used his talents (and at times his lack thereof) to produce a coherent account of what Jesus said and did.

Who Wrote It, When and Where?

TRADITION holds that the Gospel of Mark was written by the same John Mark whom we encounter in the Acts of the Apostles. We first hear about him in passing when he is mentioned in the account of how Peter escaped from prison through the intervention of an angel (Acts 12). Peter went to the house of Mary, the mother of John Mark.

The next time he appears is more significant. He accompanies Paul and Barnabas on one of their missionary journeys (Acts 12:25). For some reason John Mark left their company (Acts 13:13), something which Paul resented bitterly. He would not even accompany Barnabas on a future mission because Barnabas wanted to take John Mark along (Acts 15:37). There is some evidence, however, that the rift between John Mark and Paul was eventually healed (Col 4:10). Even if many scholars question whether Paul actually wrote this particular letter, the reference to John Mark probably reflects historic events, a reconciliation between the two.

This picture of Mark is not all that flattering. He abandoned his mission and left the others hanging. This very fact, though, gives us some important evidence to support the tradition that Mark actually wrote this Gospel. If one wanted to attribute the Gospel to an important figure in the early Church, they would have chosen someone more heroic than Mark. The very fact that

Mark was not exceptional means that he probably did write the Gospel (for no one would have said he did if he hadn't).

While tradition holds that Mark was a Disciple of St. Peter, it also holds that he was not a Disciple of Jesus. There are many who believe that the only time he followed Jesus was on the night that Jesus was arrested. He might be the young man who ran away naked when the soldiers grabbed his clothes (Mk 14:51f). This episode only appears in the Gospel of Mark and Mark probably included it as an autobiographical detail.

It was Peter, though, who provided Mark with eyewitness material which Mark then incorporated into an account along with other materials that he received from other sources. The early Fathers of the Church, however, caution us to remember that since Mark was not there himself, he was not always sure of when things happened and he put the details together as best he could.

When did Mark write his Gospel? We believe that he wrote it around 70 A.D., after the destruction of the temple in Jerusalem. Chapter 13 is so graphic in its description of the "future" destruction of the temple that it seems as if it were written right around the time that this actually occurred.

Where did he write it? Tradition holds that he wrote it in Rome, the city where his mentor, Peter, had been martyred a few years before. Mark wrote the Gospel in Greek, but there are a number of expressions that are more Latin than Greek. These are called Latinisms (much as French expressions used in English might be called "Frenchisms"). In the first century A.D., Latin was spoken mostly in Italy and North Africa. Most of the rest of the Roman Empire used Greek. Thus, this Gospel had to have been written where Latin was widely spoken, in Italy or North Africa (which gives a bit of evidence that the tradition of a Roman origin of the Gospel is valid).

What Sources Did Mark Use?

MARK, not having been a Disciple of Jesus, depended upon others for his material. One of his sources, as we have already seen, was the eyewitness account of Peter. An example of this is found in the story of Jesus' first day at Capernaum (1:21). There are so many details to the account and the presentation is so immediate that it sounds as if it is coming right out of Peter's mouth.

Another source that Mark used was an account of the Passion and death of Jesus. This account seems to have been very old, probably dating to the years immediately after Pentecost. We are not sure whether it was written down or passed on orally, but it obviously was considered to be very important material by the community. There is one interesting element to Mark's account of the Passion, though, for it seems as if certain stories contained in the narrative were added by Mark himself. These stories have Latinisms, while the rest of the account does not. If one takes those particular episodes out of the Passion narrative, it does not interrupt the flow of the material. Mark probably took the Passion narrative that he was given and inserted some other details which he learned in Rome (hence the presence of the Latinisms).

Still another source was a collection of the accounts of miracles. These stories often contained certain basic elements: 1) a description of the situation; 2) an appeal for help; 3) an action; and 4) the reaction of the people.

There were also sayings and parables of Jesus. Sayings were short passages that tell us what Jesus said in a particular situation. They were usually only a few verses long. Parables are longer accounts of Jesus' teaching. There are relatively few parables in this Gospel. Most of our favorites, in fact, are found in the Gospels of Matthew and Luke.

There are a series of stories that are often called opposition stories for they tell of the difficulties that Jesus encountered from the Pharisees and Sadducees. There are five accounts in chapters 2 and 3 that take place in Galilee and five that appear later in the Gospel that take place in Judea.

There was a liturgical source. This was material that was collected to serve a liturgical need. An example of this is the account of Jesus' baptism in the Jordan. It points out the difference between the baptism of John the Baptist (which was a baptism for the forgiveness of sins) and Christian baptism (which confers forgiveness of sin but also establishes a special relationship with God the Father, Son and Holy Spirit).

There are independent narratives that made their way into the text, e.g., the arrest and death of John the Baptist (6:17ff).

There also seems to have been a narrative that outlines the ministry of Jesus in Galilee. Mark seems to have used it as a skeleton upon which he hung his other material.

How Mark Wrote His Gospel

WHEN we try to picture in our minds how Mark and the other evangelists wrote their Gospels, we often see them sitting at great oak desks, quill pen in their hands, with the Holy Spirit or an angel whispering the words they were to write into their ears. From what we know of Mark's process, however, that is not a very accurate portrait. A much more useful image would be a high school freshman writing her first term paper. She goes to the internet and finds all the articles that have anything to do with her topic. She prints them out, takes out scissors and a glue pen and pastes together a ten-page term paper with ninety-nine foot notes. There is not all that much original material in her paper, mostly the connecting words that tie together her many sources.

Mark seems to have done something very similar with his sources. He took all the material he had and pasted it together as best he could. As one reads through the Gospel, one can still see the seams he left as he combined materials, i.e. he sometimes passes from one topic to another a little too abruptly.

But what does this say about the action of the Holy Spirit? Again, we sometimes think about the inspiration of the Holy Spirit as being a process in which the Spirit told the evangelists exactly what they were to write. Yet, when we think about the Holy Spirit's action in our own lives, we come to realize that the Holy Spirit acts through our daily events. The Holy Spirit does not impose upon us; the Spirit invites us.

There is an image that might be useful to understand the process of inspiration. At the Second Vatican Council, a Monsignor from the Eastern Rite Catholic Church rose up and proposed that inspiration be thought of in terms of the Annunciation. Msgr. Edelby said that as the Holy Spirit descended upon Mary to combine that which was divine with that which was human to produce the presence of God among us, Jesus, so also the Holy Spirit descended upon the sacred authors to combine that which was divine (inspiration) with that which was human (the authors' talent or lack thereof) to produce the presence of God among us: Sacred Scripture.

Jesus was truly God's presence among us, but He also suffered from our human weaknesses (as seen in the hymn found in Phil 2). He was like us in all things but sin. Likewise, Sacred Scripture is truly inspired, but that doesn't always mean that it is perfect. There are grammatical mistakes, small contradictions, etc.

So even if Mark compiled pre-existent verses and did not add all that much content of his own, his work was inspired. The Holy Spirit used Mark's meager talent to produce a Gospel, and although this Gospel is not perfect, it is nevertheless the Word of God.

We could even reflect upon the fact that God's Word could be proclaimed in a form that is so imperfect. Isn't this just like us? None of us is perfect. We all have our faults and we are all broken in some way. Yet, we can proclaim the Word of God in our own lives.

There is a third application to Msgr. Edelby's proposal. When we read Sacred Scripture, it is the action of the Holy Spirit that makes sure that we are not just reading a history book. It is the Spirit Who makes our experience a moment of revelation.

No Infancy Narrative

ONE of the first things that one notices about the Gospel of Mark is what is not there: an infancy narrative. One would expect that if Mark were writing a biography of Jesus, that he would include the story of His origins. Yet, his Gospel is not a true biography. It is the story of Jesus' public ministry up to His death and Resurrection. Thus, Mark begins his story with the account of John the Baptist baptizing Jesus in the Jordan River.

(This is, by the way, why Mark is represented by a lion, for his Gospel begins with John the Baptist roaring his call to conversion, much like a lion would roar out in the desert.)

While this was satisfactory for most of Mark's readers, it led to one difficulty. One of the earliest heresies in the Church was called adoptionism. Since Yahweh was God and there is only one God, early believers had a difficult time figuring out where Jesus fit in. One of the early suggestions was that at some point He was adopted to be Yahweh's Son. The logical moment for that adoption would be either the Resurrection, the Transfiguration, or the Baptism.

The idea that God would adopt a human being as His son was already part of the faith of the Jewish people. We see it in Psalm 2. When a king of Israel was enthroned, the high priest would proclaim him to be an adopted son of God, a type of viceroy for God upon the earth.

During the Baptism account in Mark, we hear that God proclaimed that Jesus was His Son. It is easy to see how the adoptionists would interpret this as being the moment when Yahweh adopted Jesus. This is certainly not what Mark meant. Yet, since his Gospel began with the baptism, one can see how it could easily be misinterpreted.

This is why the next two Gospels written, Matthew and Luke, both contain an infancy narrative. The stories of the birth of Jesus make it clear that Jesus was already God when He was conceived in the womb of the Blessed Virgin Mary. But even that was not enough, for Jesus was always God, even before He was conceived. This is why John, the last Gospel written, begins with, "In the beginning..." Jesus did not become God for He always was the Son of God in all eternity.

This development reminds us, however, that when the evangelists wrote their Gospels, they were not only telling the story of Jesus. They were also reacting to particular situations in the communities for which they were writing. This is one reason why it is so important to study the Gospels, so that we might better know why things were phrased one way or another.

Questions

1. Who wrote the Gospel of Mark and why?
2. Where did Mark find the material he used in this Gospel?
3. Was Mark a good author? A good editor?
4. Why did Mark not include an account of the birth of Jesus?

Prayer

God, You inspired St. Mark to use his meager talents to produce his beautiful Gospel. Help me to recognize that You can likewise use me and my talents, and even my brokenness, to make Your message known.

Chapter 2

Titles of Jesus

MARK begins his Gospel with the phrase, "The beginning of the Gospel of Jesus Christ, (the Son of God)." This is the first time that the word "Gospel" is being used for a written document. Before this time, it was used for the message that Jesus suffered and died for us and that He had risen from the dead. From now on, it would stand for one of the four written accounts of the life and ministry of Jesus.

Mark calls Jesus "the Christ." This is a title, not a last name. It is the Greek form of the Hebrew word "Messiah." The messiah was to be the hero whom God sent to deliver His people from all their enemies. Some accounts spoke of a kingly messiah, others of a priestly messiah. By calling Jesus "the Christ," Mark was saying that Jesus was the fulfillment of all the Old Testament promises of a deliverer.

But Jesus was not the type of messiah whom the Jewish people expected. This is why He never even used the title for Himself. Whenever someone would call Him the messiah, He would call Himself the "Son of Man." This title appears often in the Old Testament. Usually it simply means "human being," for the Hebrew form is "Ben Adam." "Ben" = "son of" and "Adam" = "man" or specifically "Adam," the first human being. So anyone who is a "Ben Adam" is a child of Adam, or a human being.

In Daniel 7, however, we hear of a mysterious figure called the Son of Man who would receive dominion over the nations. This text was written during a time of persecution of the Jews, and the title "Son of Man" probably was a reference to the Jewish people who would one day vanquish their persecutors. Yet, by the time of Jesus, it seems as if the title was being used for an individual who was to come to deliver Israel from its foes. Jesus identified Himself as that individual.

But He also qualified what He meant when He used this term. Whenever He uses "Son of Man," He also includes phrases taken from the Songs of the Suffering Servant in the Book of the Prophet Isaiah. These four songs which are used in the liturgy of Holy Week speak of a person Who would suffer meekly to bring justice to the whole world. He would take our sins upon Himself and die for us, and then He would rise from the dead. Jewish sages were not sure who this suffering servant was. Jesus said that it was He.

So when Jesus speaks of His mission, He speaks in terms of being the Son of Man Who would suffer, die, and rise in glory to rule over the nations.

A third title used for Jesus was "Son of God." We have to be a bit more careful with this term for it means one thing in the Old Testament and something different in the New Testament. In the Old Testament, it is used for the minor gods who were part of God's court (at a time when Israel still believed that many gods existed but that Yahweh was their God, a belief called henotheism). Later in Old Testament times it also was used for a hero such as a king or a prophet.

In the New Testament, it means the only begotten "Son of God." Is this how Mark means it when he uses the title? The first time that it appears is in the first verse of the Gospel. (Most translations put these words in brackets or parentheses because this phrase does not appear in all of the ancient manuscripts of this Gospel.) From its context, one can see that it is a title of honor, but it is not exactly clear what it infers.

Oddly enough, the second time that this title is used, it is proclaimed by a demon. The demon asks Jesus, "What have You to do with me, Jesus, Son of the Most High God?" The importance of this usage is that the demon is a spiritual creature who therefore knows Who Jesus is, that He is God's only begotten Son.

Finally, we hear the title again when Jesus dies on the Cross (Mk 15:39). A centurion who sees Jesus die proclaims, "Truly this man was the Son of God." It is important that this man was a centurion and not a Jew. If a Jew had said, "Son of God," it would have meant that Jesus was truly a hero. But centurions were pagans, and pagans believed that their gods could have children. Thus, when a pagan says "Son of God" under the Cross, it means the same thing that we mean when we say that Jesus is the Son of God, that the relationship between Yahweh and Jesus is one of Father and Son.

Jesus is never called "God" in this Gospel. This title, in fact, is only used twice in the New Testament for Jesus. The reason why it is used so infrequently is that Jewish people professed every day that there is only one God. If Yahweh is God, then how could Jesus also be God? Instead of calling Jesus "God," New Testament authors called Jesus "Lord." In the Old Testament, God's name was Yahweh. Yet, this name was so holy that it could not be pronounced out loud. Instead of using God's name, people would substitute another word: "Adonay." This word means "the Lord." In the Old Testament, Yahweh is therefore "the Lord." In the New Testament, since authors were hesitant to call Jesus "God," but they believed that He was God, they used the title "Lord." They were saying that Jesus was the same thing as Yahweh without using the word "God."

Mark does not use the title "Lord" for Jesus all that often. It is only used at the end of the Gospel after the Resurrection in verses that might not have been written by Mark (16:9-20). We will see why these verses are dubious later on in this book.

Thus, in the Gospel, Jesus is the Christ, the Son of God.

Question

1. What is the meaning of the titles: Son of Man, Son of God, Christ, Messiah, and Lord?

Prayer

Jesus, what should I call You? Who are You to me? Why have You shown me such incredible love and mercy?

Chapter 3

Mark the Editor

AT this point, it might be good to look at a few examples of how Mark used the cut and paste technique when he wrote his Gospel.

A first example of this technique is found in 1:40-45, the story of the healing of a leper. This is a standard miracle story with nothing all that extraordinary about it. The only question that scholars raise is, "When did it happen?" The information that immediately precedes it clearly occurred within a 24-hour period, the account of Jesus' first day at Capernaum. But there is no indication at the beginning of the story of the leper as to when it occurred in reference to the preceding material. Was it a day later, or a week later, etc.?

We have to remember that Mark often received pieces of information from his various sources. He did not always know when things occurred. This might very well be a miracle account that he knew was true and wanted to place in his Gospel, but did not know when it happened. He might have put it here to complete the thought that immediately precedes it, that Jesus was performing many miracles and this was therefore an example of those miracles. But it also prepares for the material that immediately follows it. There the scribes question Jesus' authority to forgive sins. Yet, we hear in the account of the leper that the healed man went to the leaders of the Jews to confirm his healing. They therefore knew that Jesus had the authority, but they chose to reject Him anyway. This made them guilty of much more than simple ignorance. They were consciously rejecting the truth of which they were aware. The account of the leper thus finishes the material that precedes it and prepares for what follows it.

A second example can be found in the accounts of the calling of the Disciples. The first two accounts are found in 1:16-20. We hear about the calls of Simon and Andrew and then of James and John. This material probably came from that outline of the ministry of Jesus that Mark used to form the skeleton of the first part of the Gospel. Then, in 2:13-14, we hear about the call of Levi the tax collector. If one reads the first two accounts and then immediately afterwards the call of Levi, one can hear that these three accounts were probably originally a set of three stories. Mark cut off the last of the three stories and put it in its present place. Why did he do that?

The call of Levi is found in the midst of the five stories of how the Pharisees opposed Jesus (2:1-3:6). This five-story collection reports an episode in which Jesus eats with tax collectors and others sinners. This episode was a saying. The purpose of the passage was to give Jesus the opportunity to say that He had come not for the righteous but for sinners. In its original form, it was a standard saying (meaning that it had a couple of verses to explain the situation and then a verse or two of what Jesus said). In its present form, the introduction is much longer than one would expect. Mark seems to have cut off the call of Levi story from its original context (the collection of three vocation stories) and pasted it on to this saying to form an extended introduction. Moving these particular verses here did not change their meaning, it only gave the saying a little more weight.

Finally, there is the saying contained in 2:18-22. The disciples of John the Baptist and the Pharisees asked Jesus why His disciples did not fast. Jesus answered that they could not fast while the bridegroom was there. When He was gone, they would fast. He thus taught that one of the reasons for fasting was that it is a type of ritual mourning for the loss of the bridegroom (which is why we fast on Good Friday). Just as one finds it difficult to swallow when one is in mourning, one would not eat to express grief upon the death of a loved one.

Jesus then speaks about sewing new cloth on old clothes and putting new wine in old wineskins. What does that have to do with fasting? Nothing! There is no logical connection between the situation described and Jesus' saying on clothes and wine. The best possible explanation is that this was an authentic saying of Jesus but that Mark did not know when He said it. He did not want to lose these words, so he had to find a place to put them. One wears new clothes at weddings, and one also drinks wine at weddings. Since Jesus mentioned a wedding in the original saying, maybe it was possible to put the clothes and wine saying here. This is a very tenuous connection, but no more so than many of the sayings of the rabbis for they often combined two distinct ideas based on the most tenuous of links.

These three examples show some of the techniques that Mark used when be wrote his Gospel. It shows that he was more of an editor than an author. Yet, even an editor can influence how one is to understand the material. There are a series of stories that run from 4:35-6:6 which illustrate this point.

A Series of Miracles

IN the ancient world, it was believed that there were three different types of miracles. There were nature miracles that changed the rules of nature, such as the parting of the Red Sea or the fact that the sun stood still for the Israelites when they battled their enemies under Joshua. There are exorcisms. The ancients believed that demons caused every illness. Today we might describe some of the situations reported in the Bible as mental illness or a particular disease such as epilepsy (e.g., Mk 9:14-29), but in ancient times these maladies were attributed to some form of demonic possession. Finally, there are healings. The small healing is when someone is cured of a disease, and the big healing is when someone is brought back to life.

In Mk 4:35, we hear about how Jesus was at sea in a boat with His Disciples. He fell asleep, and He did not wake up even when a serious storm blew up. His Disciples awoke Him somewhat rudely. (This scene is softened in Matthew and Luke, but Mark's version is probably closer to what originally happened for these were not gentle men.) Jesus awakes and rebukes the Disciples for their lack of faith. He then calms the wind and the waves, a miracle that filled the Disciples with a sense of awe.

There are actually two levels of meaning in this miracle. At its surface level, it is already a great nature miracle. But there is also the fact that this miracle involved the sea. The Jewish people were a desert people and they did not like the sea. They considered it to be a reservoir of evil. This was where the ancient creatures of chaos named Leviathan and Behemoth lived. This is why in the Book of Revelation there is a new heaven and a new earth, but there is no sea in heaven. If Jesus could calm the sea, then He obviously had power over the forces of evil.

The second miracle in this series occurs when Jesus reaches the shore. There He finds a man who is possessed by a very strong demon. The strength is emphasized by the fact that people had tried to bind him but were never successful. The demon recognizes Jesus, calling Him "the Son of the Most High God." Jesus asks the demon what his name is, and it answers that it is "Legion." This means that the man was possessed by many demons (again emphasizing the strength of the evil forces that Jesus was confronting). Jesus exorcises the demons from the man and sends them into a herd of swine. (There are pigs here because this is not Jewish territory. The population of this region was mostly pagan.) The swine rush off into the sea where they drown. Some people ask why Jesus killed the swine, but He didn't. The demons killed the swine.

Interestingly enough, after the man was exorcized, he wanted to follow Jesus, but Jesus refused him permission. He told him to go home and tell his family what God had done for him. Did Jesus send him back because he had been excluded from society for so long and now He wanted him to enjoy the social context of living with his family once again?

The third miracle is actually a double miracle: a small healing and a large healing. The small healing involves a woman who was suffering for twelve years from a hemorrhage (the menstrual flow). Because of her problem, she was ritually impure for all that time, excluded from contact with the community. She rushed up to Jesus and touched His clothing. This was something she should not have done for technically she was making Jesus impure as well. Instead, she found herself cured immediately. The text says that the power went out from Jesus, almost as if it were a static shock. Mark describes the miracle this way because it was not so much Jesus Who performed the miracle as the woman's faith in Him.

When Jesus feels the power go out from Him, He looks around to see who had touched Him. From the way that Mark describes it, it seems as if He didn't actually know who did it. This is typical of Mark's Gospel where we see Jesus' human limitations more clearly than in the other Gospels. Matthew and Luke have Jesus look up at the woman who was healed (for in those Gospels He knows who she is).

The other healing miracle involves the daughter of Jairus. Jesus was on His way to her, in fact, when the woman with the hemorrhage touched Him. This is a commonly used technique in Mark where one story begins, a second interrupts it, and then Mark returns to complete the first story.

Before Jesus arrives at Jairus' house, they hear that the girl had already died. Jesus insists on continuing on His way, saying that the girl was only asleep. The people who were mourning for her broke out in laughter when they heard this. (They were probably paid mourners and therefore not really all that emotionally involved in the whole affair.) Yet, Jesus' statement almost sounds like that of a small child who consoles her grieving parents by telling them that her sibling was not dead, only asleep. Jesus sees things with a childlike simplicity. He enters the room with the girl's father and mother and brings her back to life.

This miracle is not really a resurrection; it is a reanimation. Resurrection occurs when someone receives a body that no longer suffers from the limitations of this world. That person would never die again. With reanimation, the person is brought back to life, but one day that person would die again.

Another thing that one should notice is that Mark translates the phrase *"Talitha koum"* from its original Aramaic into Greek. This means that Mark intended this Gospel mostly for people who would not have understood Aramaic. It was intended for a Greek-speaking audience.

With all of these miracles one after another, one can clearly see that Jesus is capable of doing it all. He has performed a nature miracle, an exorcism, and the small and large healing.

So how do people in His hometown of Nazareth respond to all of these miraculous deeds? One would have expected them to be filled with awe and wonder. That is not the case. Instead of celebrating the revelation of God in their midst, they are offended because of what they interpret as Jesus' arrogance and presumption. They knew Him too well, and they just couldn't stand the fact that He might be more important than they were. After all the miracles that Jesus performed, they just could not embrace Him and His mission. This is why Jesus quoted the saying that a prophet is not accepted in his own homeland, by his own kin, and by his own family. While Mark quotes Jesus as saying something that could be interpreted as offensive to His own family, Matthew and Luke soften the saying by dropping the phrase referring to his family. Mark says things the way they were; Matthew and Luke try to make it more palatable (or at least not quite as embarrassing to those who might be reading these Gospels).

This tendency not to see the good in those around us is so common. We can easily see the good in others, but we sometimes only see the faults in the members of our own family.

Questions

1. How does Mark manipulate the material he received to communicate his own point of view?
2. What types of miracles are there? When Jesus "does it all," how do His family and friends respond?

Prayer

Holy Spirit of truth, help me not to ignore the signs of Your presence and authority in my life and in the world. Help me to recognize the miracles that still occur today, both the big ones and the small ones of everyday life.

Chapter 4

What Jesus Reveals about His Mission

The Messianic Secret

THESE are not the only miracles that Jesus performed. There are seventeen specific miracles mentioned in the text (in addition to all of the generic references to miracles done by Jesus).

One of the odd things about the miracles, though, is that they often end with Jesus telling people not to say anything about it. Isn't that odd? One would think that He would want everyone to hear about the miracles so that they would understand that He is the Messiah. Instead, it almost seems like He is hiding His true identity. He never even calls Himself "the Messiah." Remember, He is always calling Himself "the Son of Man." Why?

Most scholars agree that it is because He is afraid that people would misunderstand His mission. He did not come into this world to crush the Romans or to establish a political kingdom. He came here to inaugurate the Kingdom of God, or more appropriately, the Reign of God. This is when God's law and God's love would reign supreme. It is not so much found in a time or a place. It is found in the hearts of those who trust in the Lord.

This reign is inaugurated not with deeds of power, but rather with a sacrifice of love. Jesus teaches us that to be God-like, we must be willing to serve others. That is the exact opposite of what we hear in the saying, "Who do you think you are, God?" This saying implies that God is capricious and autocratic, only concerned with His own prestige. But when God comes to earth in the person of Jesus, He offers His life and death up as a sacrifice of love to bring us freedom from all those things that enslave us: selfishness, sin, loneliness, hurt, etc.

And so when Jesus performs a miracle, He tries to keep people from focusing on the wrong thing. When people hear about a possible miracle, they often flock to the site to catch a glimpse. They want to see works of wonder. But miracles are supposed to call us to generosity and service. We see this in the story of the healing of Peter's mother-in-law (1:29-31). As soon as she is healed, she gets out of bed and cooks a meal. That is the proper response to any favor we receive from the Lord: service.

The Disciples' Confusion

IT was very difficult for the Disciples to understand this. It went against everything they had ever learned. That is why, when Jesus predicted His passion three times in chapters 8, 9 and 10, they responded inappropriately.

In Mk 8:27ff, Jesus asked the Disciples who people thought He was. They gave various answers, so He asked them who they thought He was. Peter answered that He was the Christ, the Messiah.

Jesus responded to this profession of faith by predicting His passion and death. Peter was horrified. He figured that if Jesus were the Messiah, then he (Peter) would probably be the prime minister or a great general. He told Jesus to stop saying these things. Jesus turned on Peter and said, "Get behind Me Satan." One of Satan's jobs is to tempt, and that is exactly what Peter was doing, tempting Jesus to use His power for His own comfort and glory.

One chapter later, 9:30-32, Jesus predicts His Passion and death a second time. When He looks around at the Disciples and asks them what they were talking about, they respond like deer caught in headlights. That is because they were talking about whom among them was the most important. Jesus called a child into their midst and told them that whoever served a child like this was the most important. This is not the passage that says that we should become like a little child. It has to do with service. Children can't pay us back for what we do for them. If we do a favor for a rich person, we might get something out of it. Jesus was saying to serve all those people who are incapable of repaying us. Our service should be disinterested and done not because we will profit but because they need it.

One chapter later, in 10:32-34, Jesus predicts His suffering and death a third time. This time, when He is finished, James and John come up to Him and ask Him if, when He gets into

His kingdom, they can sit on His right and left. This is like telling one's friend that one is dying, and the friend responds by saying, "What a shame, but can I have your car when you're gone?"

Three times Jesus predicts His Passion, and three times the Disciples get it wrong. It is no accident that when Jesus is tempted in the desert in this Gospel (1:12-13), we do not hear about the three temptations like we do in Matthew and Luke. We don't need them. The Disciples did a good enough job on their own.

And when you think of it, isn't that the way that we are most often tempted? Very few of us receive a vision of Satan tempting us to sign a contract to sell our souls like Faust. Most of us are tempted by everyday things around us: TV, friends, food, gossip, etc.

Furthermore, the confusion of the Disciples is not limited to these three episodes. All throughout these chapters, they reach for power while Jesus preaches service. They are unable to heal the boy who was possessed (9:14-29). Jesus tells them that it can only be done through prayer. In other words, they were trying to heal the boy on their own authority instead of trusting in God. John then asks Jesus to stop a man who is casting out demons in Jesus' name (as if the Disciples were supposed to have a monopoly on this practice). They try to prevent children from coming to Jesus for a blessing (10:13-16). Peter asks Jesus what the Disciples' reward is going to be (10:25). They become indignant when James and John ask to sit on either side of Jesus in His kingdom (10:41). In all of this, they are only thinking of themselves.

Two Faith Miracles

THIS does not mean that the Disciples are evil. They just don't seem to get it. There is a miracle in chapter 8, in fact, which seems to be a symbolic way of speaking about their confusion: the healing of the blind man of Bethsaida (8:22-26). Jesus puts spittle on the man's eyes and lays His hands on him and asks him what he sees. The man answers that he sees people but that they look like walking trees. So Jesus has to lay His hands on his eyes again, and then the man sees clearly.

First of all, how did the blind man know what walking trees looked like? The text does not say that he was blind since birth. Maybe he could originally see, and he only lost his sight at some later point in his life.

Then we must ask why it took Jesus two attempts to heal the man. Didn't Jesus get it right the first time? No, this miracle represents the faith of the Disciples. This is why it immediately precedes the first prediction of the Passion. When the Disciples first came to Jesus, they thought they saw clearly. Yet, their vision was distorted. They only saw what they wanted to: what they could gain by following Jesus. It was when they experienced the cross that they came to see clearly what it meant to be a Christian. It is not about what we can get from it, it is about what we can give. This would be a good response to those who ask why they have to go to Church when they don't get anything out of it. Who said it is all about us? Maybe we should be there to give (praise and thanksgiving) rather than thinking about what we'll get out of it.

Having said that there is a symbolic meaning to this miracle in no way means that it didn't happen. It did, but Mark places it here to give it the additional symbolic meaning.

A second symbolic miracle about faith is that of the cursing of the fig tree (11:12-14, 20-21). Jesus was going into the temple sometime around the Passover. He saw a fig tree that had no fruit on it, so He cursed it. When He passed by the next day, the fig tree had dried up and withered.

This miracle doesn't seem fair. Passover is a feast that occurs in the Spring (March or April). Fig trees in Israel bear their fruit in the Fall (October). That fig tree was not supposed to have fruit. It was only doing what God had created it to do by not having fruit in the Spring. Why did Jesus curse it?

Again, it seems as if this is a symbolic miracle. The fig tree represents the Scribes and Pharisees with whom Jesus had such difficulty in these chapters. Jesus came as their Messiah, but in a manner that they hadn't expected. One could almost say that He had come "out of season," just as He did to the fig tree. They still should have been ready to accept Him and thus bear fruit. Because they were not, they were cursed. They would dry up and wither just like that fig tree. The fig tree ultimately represents all those people who refuse to make the leap of faith and trust in Jesus. At least the disciples did that, even if at first they were confused about what it meant.

Notice, there is no third miracle about people who get it right from the start. No one ever does. We all have to grow in our faith, and we all make mistakes. We all hope that God will come along and see all of our problems and solve them. Then one day we become frustrated and we ask God why He didn't make it all better. Yet, God does not come into life to make it all better, He comes into our life to make all the difference. And we usually come to realize that and learn to trust through the cross, our own crosses through which we learn the true meaning of the Christian calling, just as the disciples did.

The Family of Jesus

EVEN the family of Jesus did not fully understand who He was. We have already seen how the town's folk and even Jesus' own family had a difficult time accepting Jesus even after He had performed every type of miracle (nature, exorcisms and healings).

There is another example of their confusion in chapter 3, verses 20 to 21 and again in verses 31 to 35. In the first passage, we hear that the family of Jesus came to take Him home because they thought that He was out of His mind. Now, it is not entirely clear who the "they" is who thought that Jesus was out of His mind, but given that the family of Jesus is specifically mentioned at the end of the chapter, it would appear to include the family.

How could the family be so confused? They were Jews, and like any good Jews of the time, they had specific ideas about what the Messiah would be. They might have even believed that Jesus was the Messiah. The difficulty was that Jesus was preaching that He would suffer and die. That did not fit in with their expectations. They were certainly mistaken in their ideas, but mistakes are not always sins. Sometimes they are just mistakes.

Was the mother of Jesus, Mary, included among the family of Jesus who was confused about who Jesus was? It is uncomfortable for us to think of her being confused, and yet she was human. While she trusted in the angel's message that her son would be the Messiah, she would probably have interpreted that message in light of her cultural experience. She would have expected her son to be a powerful leader. If she was confused, it doesn't mean that she sinned. Remember how it says in Scripture that she "pondered these things in her heart." The heart, as we have seen, is where one thinks. She was thinking it over, trying to put the pieces together. Given that Jesus' ministry and His person were a great mystery, would it be unreasonable for her to have needed a bit of time to wrap her mind around what was happening?

Furthermore, doesn't this make her more available to us? When we are confused, she understands our plight. She can empathize with our struggle for she went through it herself.

In the second passage, Mary and the brothers of Jesus arrive outside the house where Jesus is staying. He is told that His mother and brothers are outside, and He looks around at those inside the room and says, "These are my mother and brothers and sisters." He is proposing that being related to Him in faith was much more important than being a relative of blood. The way that Mark phrases this, too, makes it seem as if Jesus is excluding those who were standing outside. (In the Gospel of Luke they are included, for Jesus does not look at those in the room. He says that "whoever" embraces the Word of God is part of His family, thus including those who were standing outside as well.)

We have to ask, "Who are the brothers and sisters of Jesus?" There are three theories concerning this. Catholics believe that they are cousins for in Hebrew and Aramaic, the word "brother" or "sister" can have a very extended meaning. (This is true even today for in Arabic the word "*Habibi*" could mean any relative.) In the Eastern Orthodox Church, there is a tradition that Joseph had been married and had children and had become a widower before he married Mary. This would explain why he died before the public ministry. We know this because Jesus is referred to as the "Son of Mary," something that would not have been said if Jesus' father were still alive. People would have thought of the children of Joseph's first marriage as Jesus half-brothers and half-sisters (although technically this was not true because Joseph was not Jesus' father, God was). The third tradition is that the brothers and sisters of Jesus were truly His brothers and sisters, a theory that Catholics do not accept because we believe that Mary remained a virgin throughout her entire life.

In these two passages, we see that the family of Jesus was confused. Like the Disciples, they saw things in a confused manner (like the people who looked like walking trees). It was only at the Cross that they fully understood Jesus' mission.

This is brought out even more clearly by the contrast between their confusion and the Pharisees' malicious rejection of Jesus. Remember how Mark likes to begin a story, insert a second story half way through, and then return to conclude the first story. This is what we have in this chapter. In 3:20-21, we hear about the family of Jesus. In 3:22, we hear about how the Pharisees rejected Jesus. Then we return to the family of Jesus. This is the same contrast that we saw between the man who was healed from his blindness and the fig tree story. The former represents those who are people of faith but who are still confused, while the latter represents those who are malicious in their rejection of Jesus.

The central section deals with those who think that Jesus is possessed. They accuse Him of being possessed by Beelzebul and of casting out demons with the power of demons. This is not simple confusion, it is purposeful rejection. It is also calumny, saying that they think that Jesus is evil while He is only trying to do good. Thus, their attitude is strongly contrasted with that of the family of Jesus which was only confused.

There are a couple of details in the story that should be explained. The scribes speak of Beelzebul. Baal was the main god worshiped by the Canaanites. There was a shrine to Baal in Zebub and that god was therefore called Baal-Zebub. The Jewish people rejected the existence of that god, so they mocked him by calling him Baalzebul (or Beelzebul). Baal-zebub meant the Lord of the town Zebub, while Baal-Zebul meant Lord of the Flies. (This might explain why flies were often associated with the demonic presence.)

A second thing that needs an explanation is the phrase "sin against the Holy Spirit." What is it, and why can't it be forgiven?

The Holy Spirit is the love between the Father and the Son. It is through the action of the Holy Spirit that we receive forgiveness for our sins. God's love cancels out the self-hate which has entered our life through our sins. Pope John Paul II said that there are two forms of the sin against the Holy Spirit. The first is to believe that our sins cannot be forgiven. One of the ironies of growing older is that we can't remember if we took our pills this morning, but we can remember the sins we committed thirty years ago, even if we confessed them long ago. If we believe that our sins can't be forgiven, then we can't accept the forgiveness that God is offering. The problem is not that God is unwilling to forgive us, it is that we won't accept the forgiveness that God is offering. How can one break out of this difficulty? One simply must accept the forgiveness that God is offering. One has to remember that God's mercy is always stronger than our sin.

A second form of the sin against the Holy Spirit is presumption, choosing to sin because one is planning to go to confession later and feels that God will have to forgive them. In this case, one is not really interested in forgiveness but is only trying to play a game with God. Again, the problem is not God, it is us. We are not really opening our hearts to God's love and mercy because we are just trying to get away with a fast one.

Questions

1. Why does Jesus not want to be proclaimed as the Messiah?
2. If I were one of the Disciples, how would I respond to Jesus' call to the cross?
3. Am I like the blind man healed by Jesus or like the fig tree? Am I like the Disciples and family of Jesus, or like the Pharisees?
4. Who were the brothers and sisters of Jesus?
5. What does Pope John Paul II tell us about the sin against the Spirit?

Prayer

God, give me the faith to proclaim You as the Lord of my life. Strengthen me when my faith wavers. Teach me to trust in You.

Chapter 5

Faith and Seeds

THE difficulty of understanding the mystery of our Christian calling comes out in the parables about seeds in chapter 4. Jesus used parables based upon things that His listeners would understand. Since most of them were farmers, He drew many of His examples from agriculture.

At the beginning of chapter 4, He speaks of seed that had fallen on the footpath, on rocky ground, among thorns, and on good soil. Jesus told His Disciples that the seed was the Word of God. He then goes on to explain the meaning of the various places where the seed was sown.

To understand His examples, one must remember the commandment that one is to love God with all of one's heart, all of one's soul, and all of one's strength. When the rabbis were asked what this meant, they responded that to love the Lord with all of one's heart is to love the Lord with one's entire intellect. In the Bible, the heart is where one thinks (not the brain). One feels with one's guts. The seed that fell on the footpath stood for those who had heard the Word of God, but Satan came and carried them off. They had not interiorized the Word in their minds (hearts).

To love the Lord with all of one's soul meant to love the Lord in a time of persecution, until they ripped one's soul right out of one's body. This was represented by the seed that fell on rocky soil. It sprouted but was rootless, and when persecution came along it faltered.

To love the Lord with all of one's strength meant to love the Lord with all of one's possessions. This is represented by the seed sown among thorns. When anxieties and cares for one's wealth came along, this seed was choked and died.

It was only the seed that fell on good soil that bore fruit many fold. The good soil was a heart and mind open and receptive.

This parable answers the question of why so few embrace the Word of God. God's Word is powerful and effective, and one would expect people to want it to be a part of their lives. One would expect them to do almost anything necessary to be one with it. But so few people accept it, and some of those who do later fall away. Why? Because people had not loved the Lord and the Word with their whole hearts, souls and strength.

In 4:12, Jesus says something unusual that is often misunderstood. He says that He preaches in parables so that "they will stare and not see, listen intently and not understand, lest perhaps they repent and be forgiven." It almost sounds as if Jesus does not want people to understand, but that is not the case. He preaches in parables to make things as clear as possible to His audience so that they will have no excuse if they reject it. Yet, Jesus knows that many will in fact refuse to accept the message. They don't want to convert, so they will not, no matter what He says.

The second seed parable is found in 4:26-29. It speaks of how the seed grows. The farmer plants the seed, but he has no idea how it actually grows. This is how the kingdom of God grows. God plants the seed of His Word in our hearts, and it grows in mysterious ways. We cannot force people to have faith; it is a gift from God. Some people have been given a greater share of the gift, others less. How does the reign of God dawn and grow upon the earth? How does God decide who gets more faith and who less? It is all beyond our understanding.

This is what St. John of the Cross wrote about in his book *The Dark Night of the Soul*. We tend to understand "the dark night" as a time of depression when all seems to be black for us. But this is not the meaning of the Spanish word "*oscura*" that we most often translate as "dark." A better translation is "hidden." God tends to work in our souls in hidden ways, in ways that are beyond our comprehension. We suddenly understand something on a spiritual level that never made sense before. We learn to surrender our will to God's at a level that we didn't think was possible. We receive a consolation one day even though we had said that same prayer for months and years and had never experienced that consolation before. We cannot force God's actions, we can only prepare ourselves so that we can respond to God's promptings when they happen. Our spiritual life is ultimately in God's hands, not ours.

Finally, there is the parable of the mustard seed (4:30-34). The Kingdom of God does not dawn upon the earth fully developed. It takes time, and it most often begins in small, seemingly insignificant ways. One person forgives another; one person reaches out in love to someone who feels unlovable; one person trusts God in the midst of suffering. It is in these small things that God's love is experienced, and love is contagious. A person who is loved then loves others, and that person loves still others, etc., until God's reign conquers hate and evil and fear.

This parable would certainly be a response for those who could not understand why the Reign of God was taking so long to manifest itself. It also spoke to those people who were scandalized that even within the Christian community things were not perfect. Why was it all taking so long?

Questions

1. Why would Jesus use seeds and sowing as a symbol in His parables?
2. How do you experience God's reign on earth?

Prayer

Lord, let my heart be fertile ground for a harvest of faith and good works. Let me not be too anxious about the difficulties of life and what I possess, lest the soil of my heart become too rocky or infertile and not be willing to receive Your Word.

Chapter 6

Jesus Lives and Dies for Us

The Resurrection Narrative

EVEN the story of Jesus' Resurrection presents a very realistic portrait of our faith life. To study this passage, though, we have to do a bit of textual criticism. This is the science of examining whether all the verses of a book were originally a part of it.

Chapter 16 presents a considerable difficulty. In many editions of the Bible, one sees references to a shorter ending and a longer ending of the Gospel. The shorter ending goes from 16:1 to 16:8. It is found in all of the ancient manuscripts. It is consistent with the rest of the Gospel in vocabulary, grammar and theology. Verses 16:9 to 16:20, the longer version, is not found in a number of important manuscripts. It is different from the rest of the Gospel in vocabulary, grammar and theology. Given this, it is logical to conclude that the longer ending was probably added to the original ending of the Gospel by a scribe. The longer ending is, in fact, an amalgamation of the Resurrection stories of the other Gospels.

If one reads the shorter ending (16:1-8), it immediately becomes obvious why the longer ending was added. The original account ends with the women hearing about the Resurrection, but they do not see the risen Jesus. They go away afraid and do not tell anyone about what they had seen and heard. Isn't this a terrible ending to a Gospel? Why would Mark have ended the Gospel this way?

There are various theories why he did this. Maybe he lost the last page of the Gospel on the way to the "printer." Maybe he died or was arrested before he finished the Gospel. Isn't that melodramatic? One can see the scroll on which Mark was writing, and there is a line of ink that runs down the scroll which was made when Mark was dragged away from his writing table.

The most likely proposal for why Mark ended his Gospel this way is that he did it on purpose. He was writing for a community of Christians in Rome who were facing martyrdom. When one is about to die, one wants Jesus to come down on a fiery chariot to rescue one from the beasts. But that doesn't happen all that often. Mark is telling his community not to expect to see the risen Jesus until after their own deaths. Just like the women, they would have to believe what they had heard and not seen. Furthermore, the fear of the women reminds us that we sometimes are faced by situations that fill us with fear and confusion. Those feelings are natural. They are not sins, they are only emotions.

Now it would be good to look at 16:1-8. The account begins with the women going to the tomb very early on Easter morning. From the way that the account describes the time of the day, it would seem that it was when one can see a glow on the horizon but one cannot yet see the disk of the sun.

This would be why the Book of Revelation speaks of the Morning Star. The Morning Star is the planet Venus which rises just before the dawn. Venus in classical mythology was the goddess of love and victory. Jesus defeated the forces of hate and death by rising from the dead just before the dawn. Thus, the morning star in the Book of Revelation is the power of the resurrection. Later in the history of the Church, the title "Morning Star" was applied to the Blessed Virgin Mary for she arose before the dawning of her Son, Jesus.

How many women were there on the first Easter morning? In the Gospel of Mark, there are three women. In John there is one. In Matthew there are two, and in Luke there are a number of women. There is only one woman in John, Mary Magdalene, because she represents the Church looking for her beloved. In Matthew, there are two because one needs two people to give witness in the Bible. In Luke, there are many because Luke strongly emphasizes the role of women in the early Christian community. In Mark there are three women because that is how many there were. Remember, Mark tends to tell things just as they occurred.

When the women reach the tomb, they encounter a young man dressed in white. This is obviously an angel, but Mark describes him this way to tie him to the young man who lost his clothes when Jesus was arrested. This could be a baptismal symbol. When we die with Christ in Baptism, we take our clothes off. When we rise with Christ, we are vested in white. The color white is not a symbol of purity in the New Testament; it is a symbol of the power of the Resurrection.

The presence of the young man could also point to a symbolic message about Mark himself. Remember the story of his life. He messed up when he left Paul and Barnabas during their missionary journey. Only later was he forgiven by Paul and given the opportunity to become a disciple of Peter. He was given a second chance. He was like the young man who ran away (which might have, in fact, been Mark) but who then gave witness to the Resurrection. Mark might have been reminding his readers that God gives us a second chance in life.

What Did Jesus Know?

WE have seen that Mark presents Jesus in the weakness of the human condition. He emphasizes the "emptying Himself of His divine prerogatives" that one hears in the hymn found in Philippians 2. Yet, Jesus was also God. How much did He know about His mission and Who He was?

Mark doesn't really delve into that question too deeply. Yet, he does make some statements that help us to establish some parameters concerning Jesus' knowledge. In 13:32 we hear Jesus say that He doesn't know when the end of the world would occur (for only the Father knows), so He obviously doesn't know everything. Furthermore, Jesus makes a factual error in 2:26 when He speaks of how Abiathar gave the bread dedicated to the Lord to David when he was fleeing from King Saul. This is wrong. Abiathar did not give David the bread, it was Abiathar's father, Ahimelech. Could Jesus make a mistake? Remember, mistakes are not sins; they are simply errors. This is important to call to mind when we begin to feel guilty for our mistakes and conclude that the guilt is an indication that we have committed a sin. Sometimes we feel guilty because things did not turn out the way we would have hoped they would. To be a sin, our choices must be conscious choices to do what we know is wrong.

In spite of these passages which demonstrate Jesus' lack of knowledge, there are others that show that He knew what His mission was and He fully embraced it. In chapters 8 to 10, we saw Him predict His passion three times. Some scholars have questioned whether He really said these things. They suggest that this was just the evangelists putting words in Jesus' mouth.

This theory can be shown to be incorrect. In 12:1-12, we hear the parable of the tenants. A man rents out his vineyard to tenants who then refuse to pay him what they owe. He sends servants to collect the rent, but they beat them up or kill them. The servants represent the prophets whom the people of Israel often mistreated. The owner then sends his own son. The tenants decided to kill the son so that they might steal the inheritance. They kill him inside the vineyard and then throw his body outside.

There is a small detail in this parable that does not coincide with what actually happened to Jesus. Jesus was not killed inside the city walls; He was killed outside of them. This inconsistency is very fortunate for us. If this parable had been created by the evangelists after the Ascension, then they would have gotten all of the details right. The very fact that one of the details does not coincide with what happened tells us that this parable was proclaimed before these things actually happened.

If Jesus was thus capable of predicting His Passion and death through this parable, then He obviously was able to do it in the other predictions of the Passion as well. In other words, Jesus knew what He was doing. We see this again when Jesus institutes the Eucharist. He speaks of His blood being poured out for many. These words are taken from the Songs of the Suffering Servant. Jesus knew that the Eucharist was a foreshadowing of Jesus' death upon the Cross.

The Last Supper

IT would be good now to look at the Last Supper. In 14:12, we hear that Jesus was preparing for the Passover. In the Synoptic Gospels (Mt, Mk and Lk), there is only one Passover. In John, there are three (which is why we speak of a three-year public ministry). Furthermore, in the synoptics, Jesus actually eats the Passover meal on the night of the first day of Passover. In John, Jesus and the Disciples anticipate the meal by a day (which the rabbis permitted because there were so many pilgrims in Jerusalem during the Passover that there was not enough room for all of them to celebrate the feast on the same evening).

Jesus tells His Disciples to look for a man carrying a jar of water. This helps us pinpoint where the meal was eaten. In most Jewish families, women would carry the water from the well. There was, however, a sect of Jews called the Essenes. The main community of Essenes was located near the Dead Sea at a place called Qumran, but there also seems to have been a smaller community of Essenes living in Jerusalem. They were very strict on purity laws, and since women were periodically impure because of menstruation, men would bring water from the wells. So if the hall is marked by a man carrying a water jar, it must have been in the Essene quarter of the city (something that has been confirmed by recent archaeological discoveries).

At the beginning of the meal, Jesus predicts that one of them would betray Him and He says that it would have been better that he had never been born. This does not necessarily mean that He is saying that Judas is going to Hell, only that he would have to live with his guilt for all eternity. (God, of course, was willing to forgive Judas, but could Judas forgive himself?) Even Judas' suicide does not guarantee that he is in Hell, for we don't know what flashed through his mind as he was taking his life. There is a possibility that he expressed perfect contrition to God.

Jesus took the bread and called it His body. The Aramaic word that He used was probably one that meant that the bread was His very self.

He also took a cup of wine (probably the third of four cups that form part of the Passover ritual). He said that it was His blood of the covenant. The blood of an animal was always shed when a covenant was established. The technical term for marking a covenant was, in fact, the cutting of a covenant. Instead of the blood of an animal, however, Jesus was offering His own blood. In Luke and 1 Corinthians, this phrase is softened a bit because they speak of the cup of the covenant in His blood. In

Mark and Matthew, there is blood in the cup, in Luke and 1 Corinthians, there is covenant in it. Jesus probably used the more graphic form found in Mark and Matthew.

Jesus also says that the blood is shed "for many." This does not mean that Jesus' blood is shed for many but not for everyone. In Hebrew and Aramaic, the phrase "for many" actually means "for everyone."

We then hear Jesus predict Peter's denial. One has to remember that Peter was one of the major sources for Mark's material. Who is it who told Mark about the denial and other embarrassing passages concerning Peter's mistakes? It was Peter himself. He was willing to tell the community about his shortcomings to teach them about God's mercy. God does not call those who are perfect; He chooses flawed individuals to carry out the mission.

This tendency to air their dirty laundry also helps affirm our belief in the testimony contained in these Gospels. Some people say that the Disciples made it all up. If they had, wouldn't they have made themselves look a little bit better in their accounts? The very fact that they willingly share their brokenness helps us believe that they are telling the whole truth about what happened.

The Trial and Passion

IT is now time to look at Jesus' trial and Passion. First of all, 14:53ff speaks of a trial before the Sanhedrin. There is a difficulty with this, for the Sanhedrin was not allowed to meet at night. Most probably, this was a meeting of the chief priests and some of the other leaders of the Jews but not of the whole Sanhedrin.

Then there is the question of why they put Jesus to death. The leaders of the Jews accuse Him of wanting to destroy the temple and rebuild it in three days. He actually did say this, but He was not speaking about the temple in Jerusalem. He was speaking about His own body. He did, though, predict the destruction of the temple in chapter 13. This was not really a crime. Jeremiah and the other prophets had predicted the destruction of the temple in their own days. It wasn't even a crime to proclaim oneself as the Messiah (although we should remember that Jesus carefully avoided that particular title). There were a number of individuals who made that claim. What He actually was convicted of was of attributing to Himself divine prerogatives, things that could be done by God alone (e.g., forgiving sins). But there was another reason why the leaders of the Jews put Jesus on trial. On Palm Sunday, He had entered Jerusalem to the acclaim of the crowd. They were proclaiming Him as the Son of David. This was an incredibly dangerous thing to do at Passover time. Jerusalem was not all that large of a city. It only had a population of about 60,000 people. At Passover time, another 250,000 people arrived to celebrate the feast in the city. The city was overcrowded and tensions were high. This is why the Roman procurator Pilate had brought some of his troops up from Caesarea by the Sea for the feast: to keep an eye on the crowd and crush any riot or rebellion before it got out of hand. Interestingly, even more nervous than the Romans were the leaders of the Jews for they had the most to lose if there was a rebellion. They would be the first to lose their privileges and riches.

When the crowd proclaimed Jesus to be the Son of David, they were saying that He should be their king. Riding into Jerusalem on a young donkey, He fulfilled the prophecy in Zechariah (9:9) concerning how the Messiah would ride into Jerusalem. Even if He never said that He was the Messiah out loud, He was proclaiming it in this symbolic action.

As if this was not enough, He then cleansed the temple. Today we would call this action "disturbing the peace." He could have started a riot. The leaders of the Jews saw Him as a dangerous man politically as well as religiously.

Jesus was taken to Pilate, the procurator of Judea. The Jews did not have the authority to put Him to death. Each of the Gospels portray Pilate differently. Mark's version has Pilate not really wanting to kill Jesus but forced to do so by the leaders of the Jews who had incited the crowd to violence.

Pilate does offer to free either Jesus or Barabbas as a Passover pardon of a prisoner. This Barabbas was probably a Zealot who had killed and robbed (which explain the various descriptions of his crimes in the four Gospels). Some scholars have asked whether his name might be symbolic (for in Aramaic *Bar* means "son of" and *abbas* means "father"). They ask whether it is a choice between Jesus, the Son of Man, and Barabbas, the son of the father. Yet, none of the Gospels emphasizes this, so it probably is just a coincidence. What is really happening is that the crowd chose a murderer over the author of life.

The soldiers beat Jesus before they took Him out to be crucified. This was normal practice for the Romans. Archaeologists have even found an inscription on a floor in Jerusalem which speaks of making prisoners "a king for a day." This was a way to humiliate and depersonalize the prisoner.

During their tortures, the soldiers put a crown of thorns on Jesus' head. This crown didn't look like the ring of thorns that we often see in artistic representations of the crucifixion. It was more of a cap that covered Jesus' entire head.

They also put a purple robe on Him. It is interesting that Mark and John call it a purple robe and Matthew calls it a scarlet robe. It is difficult for us to understand how the soldiers would have had access to a purple robe. Purple was the color used by the royal family. It was very, very expensive. Scarlet would make more sense for that was the color worn by centurions. That would have been readily available. Yet, Mark and John don't agree on much, and they both speak of the robe being purple. No matter how improbable it seems to us, the robe probably was purple.

On the way to Golgotha, Jesus was assisted by Simon of Cyrene. We hear that he was the father of Alexander and Rufus. This is the only Gospel which mentions the names of Simon's two sons. They were probably members of the early Christian community.

Jesus is led to the hill called Golgotha which is translated as "the place of the skull." Notice that it is translated into Greek just like the phrase *"Talitha koum."* Golgotha was a mound of rock that lie in an inactive rock quarry. The mound had been left there because it had a natural flaw that made it unusable. It was called Golgotha because it looked something like a skull. The upright portion of the cross was probably stuck in the flaw (the crack in the rock). This is why the psalm verse, "the stone rejected by the builders has become the cornerstone," was so important in the early Church.

We hear that Jesus was given wine mixed with myrrh. In ancient times, wine tended to be stored in a concentrated form. People often mixed perfumes like myrrh in with the wine to improve its taste. Matthew, instead of speaking of myrrh, speaks of gall mixed with wine. Gall was wormwood, and it would have had an hallucinogenic effect, deadening the pain.

Mark says that the crucifixion occurred at nine in the morning while the other Gospels speak of that happening at noon. They had no watches in those days, so it was probably sometime between nine and noon.

Mark mentions the two men who were crucified with Jesus. Here they are called revolutionaries (which does not preclude their being thieves as well). There is no good thief in Mark. That account only appears in Luke.

We do not know what it means when it says that darkness covered the whole land. Was it an eclipse or clouds covering the sun or some other form of darkness? Was it the whole earth, or the land of Israel, or the area around Jerusalem? The text is not all that clear.

We hear about the abuse hurled upon Jesus. This is found in all of the Gospel accounts.

When Jesus says, "My God, my God, why have You abandoned Me," He was quoting Psalm 22. On the one hand, He is expressing His feelings of abandonment. While He trusted the Father, He also felt abandoned. Yet, since Psalm 22 is a lamentation, it ends like all other lamentation psalms. It ends with a short hymn of praise to celebrate what the Psalmist was sure would be his liberation. By citing the first verse, Jesus is actually citing the entire psalm, including the hymn of praise.

In this Gospel, Jesus does not commend His spirit. He simply breathes His last.

Finally, the veil in the temple split from the top to its bottom. The veil separated the Holy of Holies from the rest of the temple. This was the most sacred part of the temple and the veil closed off the holy space from where the faithful could enter. Now, the holiness of God was crashing out into the world. God could be encountered in the everyday world. This is why our seven sacraments are made of such everyday things: words, bread, wine, oil, breath, and touch.

Questions

1. What is unusual about the end of Mark's Gospel?
2. Did Jesus know everything? Did He know anything? Where is the balance between these two extremes?
3. What is the significance of Jesus calling the bread His body and the wine His blood?
4. Why is Mark's version of the Passion so stark? How does that fit in with his larger message?

Prayer

Jesus, teach me to carry my cross and to die to myself so that I might die and rise with You. Help me to see that mystery every time I participate in the celebration of the Mass.

Chapter 7

Other Passages that Give Insight into Jesus and Mark

CHAPTER 13 speaks of the devastation of the temple in Jerusalem and the end of the world. It is very apocalyptic in nature. The apocalyptic style speaks of heavenly interventions by angels, cataclysmic events, etc. It appears in the Old Testament books like Daniel, Ezekiel and Joel. In the New Testament, we find the Book of Revelation which is entirely apocalyptic. There are apocalyptic chapters in 1 and 2 Thes, the Gospels, etc. It is a way of describing the events that would occur at the end of time. It is doubtful that apocalyptic authors intended for their writings to be taken literally. Like parables which use symbolic language, so also apocalyptic language is symbolic.

This doesn't mean that there won't be an end of time. We believe that this world will not last forever. Some day it will end.

Will there be a time of tribulation before the end of the world? One could make a good argument that we are already living in the end times. There is always a price to pay for being faithful Christians. We have to take up our crosses and follow Jesus wherever He leads us. Will there be another period of purification that comes before the end, or is this just symbolic language? This is not all that clear.

When will the end occur? According to this Gospel, Jesus neither knew when the end would come nor did He want us to know. We are supposed to always be ready. Whenever there is a natural disaster or war, some people immediately say that it is a sign of the end of the world. Besides, what is the greatest sign of the end times? Gray hair! It is a reminder that we will not live forever and we should always be ready for the end (whether it be the end of the world or our own personal end).

Besides, we should look forward to the end. We want to be with Jesus. We want to be in heaven (only if we are honest, most of us would say that we wouldn't mind waiting a bit before the end comes).

Jesus and the Pharisees

WE have already seen that one of the sources for this Gospel was a series of opposition stories. One of the groups which consistently opposed Jesus was the Pharisees. Who were they?

Pharisees were dedicated Jewish laymen who believed that the law was such a precious gift from God that it should be practiced to the letter. They, in fact, went even further for they tried to "build a fence around the law." This meant to take the law to its widest possible interpretation just to make sure that they were not breaking the smallest part of the law.

While their dedication is admirable, they tended to become legalistic and judgmental. Their interpretation of the law was called the tradition of the Fathers. Jesus objected to many of their interpretations for He felt that it made the obligations of the law onerous. He also accused them of hypocrisy, saying that they kept the external regulations while they did not allow their hearts to be transformed by God's love, e.g., 7:1-23.

The Pharisees, for their part, tried to trap Jesus by posing difficult if not impossible problems. They and the Herodians, for example, asked Him whether they should pay taxes to the emperor (12:13-17). This was an obvious trap. If He said yes, He would be accused of collaboration with the Romans, the occupying power. If, on the other hand, He said that they should not pay the taxes, then they could accuse Him of insurrection and have the Romans arrest Him. Jesus sidestepped the issue by saying that they should give to God what is God's and to Caesar what is Caesar's. All through the New Testament, though, there was a debate as to what belonged to God and what belonged to the state (a debate that continues to the present day).

The Sadducees also tried to trick Jesus. Sadducees were the survivors of the Jewish royal family, the high priest, and many of the other leaders of the Jews. The Sadducees were traditionalists. They only believed that the first five books of the Bible were normative (for them everything else was spiritual reading). They did not believe in angels or messengers from God, nor did they believe that God had a special purpose for their lives. They also did not believe in the resurrection of the dead.

Throughout most of the Old Testament, Jewish people did not believe in the resurrection of the dead. They believed that when one died, one went to Sheol. This was a place of shades. There was no joy, no emotion. We hear that when an important person died, those in Sheol only commented, "Oh, he is dead." One could not even pray in Sheol. Furthermore, everyone went to Sheol: good, bad and indifferent. It is not a place of punishment. It is simply the fate of all human beings.

Where was one rewarded for being a good person? It had to be in this life. If one was a good person, then one lived a long and healthy life. If one were evil, then one died early and miserable.

This is an interesting theory, but it doesn't match reality. Some wicked people live long and prosperous lives; some good people die young and miserable. There is even a saying, "Only the good die young."

Because this theory of reward and punishment was so unreliable, Jewish theologians began to look for another theory on the afterlife. Some time around the exile (587 B.C.), they began to speak of the resurrection of the dead (possibly even borrowing this idea from surrounding cultures). But not all Jews accepted this theory. The Sadducees are an example of those who did not believe in the resurrection of the dead.

In 12:18-27, the scribes set their trap. They speak of the law that the widow of a man who had no descendants was to marry the next of kin. If a woman married seven brothers, one after the other, they asked whom she would belong to in the resurrection of the dead. For them, this was intended as an absurd example that would show how silly it was to believe in the resurrection of the dead.

Jesus answers their challenge in two ways. First of all, He tells them that in the life to come, she won't "belong" to anyone. We will be like angels, not having the same types of relationships that we have here on earth. This does not mean, however, that we will not be with those whom we love. In heaven, we will be like God, and thus we will love people without any of the limitations to our love from which we suffer here on earth, e.g., jealousy.

Jesus then reaffirms His belief in the resurrection of the dead by citing the creedal formula that God is the God of Abraham,

Isaac and Jacob. If these people were dead and gone, then why would one mention their names. One would be saying that Yahweh was the God of non-existent entities. So, according to Jesus, these patriarchs must still be alive. Those who are dead do not cease to exist, they have a share in God's life in another way than they did while they were here on earth. Furthermore, in heaven we will have bodies (this is the meaning of the resurrection). Our bodies, though, will be glorified bodies that do not suffer from the limitation of these present bodies (e.g., weakness, illness, etc.).

Jesus' Teaching on Divorce

AT times, Jesus was the One Who did the challenging. Jesus' teaching on divorce is a good example of this. Jewish law allowed a man to divorce his wife (but not the other way around). What were some of the grounds for divorce? Adultery was one of the grounds, and another was if the woman displeased her husband.

Around the time of Jesus, there were rabbis who reflected upon the law. The most famous rabbis during this era were Hillel and Shemei. Hillel was famous for extending the law to make it easier to observe, Shemei the exact opposite.

When Hillel developed his commentary on divorce, he made it easier for men to divorce their wives (which obviously was not that good for the women). What did adultery mean for Hillel? He said that if a woman went to market and one could see her ankle or her elbow, then it was as if she were naked, and if she were naked, it was as if she had committed adultery. What would it mean that a wife displeased her husband? Hillel answered that it was enough if she burned his supper once. That was enough to be grounds to divorce a wife.

Jesus rejected Jewish teaching on divorce (cf 10:1-12). He taught that divorce was wrong. There were two reasons for this. First of all, Jesus treated women with respect (remember His teaching on resurrection and how women do not "belong" to anyone when they are in heaven). Divorce treated women as property, and so Jesus rejected it.

Furthermore and more importantly, He spoke of the fact that marriage is a covenant in which two become one. One should not separate what God has joined together. This is the same teaching that one can find in Mal 2:13ff.

The Faith of Non-Jews

ONE of the surprising things one finds in this Gospel (both for us and for the Jews of Jesus' days) was how non-Jews responded to His ministry. While the leaders of the Jews rejected Him and the Disciples were confused about Him, we hear about non-Jews who came to believe in Him.

The Syro-Phoenician woman is a good example of this (7:24-30). Tyre and Sidon lie to the northwest of Galilee and they were considered to be pagan territory. A woman who was a pagan came up to Jesus and asked Him to cast a demon out of her daughter. Jesus answered her in a somewhat rude manner, saying that it was not right to give the children's food to the dogs. Dogs were considered to be unclean by the Jews for they ate carrion. Was Jesus insulting her because He was using a saying common in His culture, or was He testing her?

What is the woman's response? She was clever enough to say that even the dogs get some of the scraps from the table. This response probably provoked a smile on Jesus' face. The woman's faith was strong enough for her to challenge Jesus.

This raises the question of how one should pray. Catholics tend to be very submissive in their prayers, leaving it to God to decide what is best. The people of this time were a bit more insistent. One of the psalms could be paraphrased as, "Lord, I am sick. You better heal me quick because if I die, then it's going to look bad for You." The Syro-Phoenician woman's response to Jesus suggests that maybe we can be a bit more insistent in some of our prayers. Of course, the final decision is always in God's hands.

After the episode of the Syro-Phoenician, we hear the story of the healing of the deaf man in Decapolis (another pagan territory). This episode is contrasted with the episode in which the Pharisees demand a sign from Jesus (8:11ff) and Jesus warns

His Disciples about the leaven of the Pharisees (8:14ff). While pagans were ready to believe, Jesus' own people were skeptical.

It is quite significant that Jesus would even have anything to do with non-Jews. The Pharisees taught that pagans were unclean for they had no way to be freed from their sins. Jews, on the other hand, could offer sacrifices in the temple to receive forgiveness for their sins. The sinfulness of the pagans was considered to be a type of contagion which could poison one if one ate or even had contact with a pagan. Remember how the leaders of the Jews would not even enter the Praetorium during Jesus' trial in the Gospel of John because they wanted to be pure for their Passover meal that evening.

Two Multiplications

JESUS' interest in the pagans could also explain why there are two multiplications of loaves and fish in this Gospel. The first one is for the 5,000. This was for Jewish people. When the fragments are gathered together, there was enough to fill twelve baskets, enough for the twelve tribes of Israel. The second multiplication is for 4,000 people and this one occurs on pagan territory. At the end of the meal, they gather up seven baskets of fragments. Seven is the perfect number in the Bible (for the ancients believed that there were seven planets and so to say "seven" was to speak of the whole universe). Thus, we see that Jesus nourishes both Jews and Gentiles.

While we are looking at these multiplications, we should consider some of the symbolism in the accounts. In the multiplication for the 5,000 (6:34ff), we hear that the crowd reclined on the green grass. Why did the evangelist specifically talk about the "green grass?" It is because the account has allusions to Psalm 23: "The Lord in my Shepherd." In that psalm, we hear that the Lord would lead the flock to verdant pastures. The green grass of the account refers to those verdant pastures. In case one missed the symbolism, the next account fulfills the next verse of the psalm that the shepherd would lead the flock to restful waters. Immediately after Jesus multiplies the loaves and fish,

He takes a walk on the waters and calms the sea (hence the restful waters).

While we are looking at this account, we should address one interpretation of the episode. Some people say that this was really a social miracle. In this interpretation, Jesus shared all the food that He had, and everyone else was moved by His generosity and shared all the food that they had. This is a beautiful interpretation, but it is just not what is contained in this passage. This is a nature miracle, like the story of the calming of the sea in chapter 4. Jesus was performing a miracle that changed the rules of the natural world. Just in case one missed the point, we immediately see another nature miracle when Jesus walks on the water. The people who give us the pot luck theory of the multiplication of loaves and fish suggest that maybe Jesus knew where the rocks were in the water. Jesus can do miracles and does them all throughout the Gospels (just as He continues to do today).

The Transfiguration

THE fact that Jesus could perform miracles is again seen in the story of the Transfiguration (9:2-8). Jesus takes His three principal Apostles (Peter, James and John) up the mountain. All throughout the Old Testament, mountains were considered to be holy places where one encountered the power of God. One of the titles for Yahweh in the Old Testament, in fact, is *El Elyon.* Today this title is often translated as "God the Most High," but it originally meant "God of the heights." Every mountain and hill in Israel had an altar to Yahweh (and unfortunately to other gods as well).

On top of the mountain, Jesus appeared in the glory of His divinity. The text strongly emphasizes how white and glowing He was. Remember, white in the New Testament did not stand for purity as much as for the glow and illumination of divinity and the power of the Resurrection.

Moses and Elijah appear on the mountain. Moses is the father of the law, having received the commandments on Mount Sinai. Elijah represents the prophets. Thus, Jesus is seen as the fulfillment of the law and the prophets. These two particular individuals appear because they both had unusual ends to their lives. Moses died and was buried by God Himself on Mount Nebo. Elijah was carried up into the heavens in a fiery chariot. Thus, both of them experienced an unusual end and were thus available to return to give witness to Jesus.

Peter offers to build three tents on the mountain. His reaction is typical of someone who encounters the holy. When we experience the holy, half of us wants to draw closer and half of us is filled with awe and fear. We want to draw closer because we are fascinated and want to see what is going on. The other reaction is fear because we realize that God is so great and we are so insignificant. This is what fear of God means. It is not to be afraid of God (as if He were going to punish us for something we did). It is to be filled with a sense of wonder. Peter wants to be there, but he is also confused as to what he should say.

There is also a cloud covering them. Remember how a cloud overshadowed the Tent of Sanctuary whenever God appeared to His people in the Old Testament. Then a voice comes from the cloud and says, "This is My beloved Son. Listen to Him." This is the same proclamation that we heard at Jesus' Baptism.

The Transfiguration then ends and Jesus and the Apostles come down from the mountain. He orders them not to say anything until the Son of Man rises from the dead, something that they did not understand.

The Disciples then ask Jesus what it meant that Elijah would have to come first. This had been predicted in Mal 2:3f. In this passage, Jesus tells the Disciples that Elijah had indeed come, implying that John the Baptist was the new Elijah. It is interesting that in the New Testament there are passages where John the Baptist is presented as Elijah, and there are others where Jesus Himself is the new Elijah (for He, too, prepared God's people for the Day of the Lord).

The story of the Transfiguration provides a reflection upon our own spiritual life. Every once in a while, we receive a gift from the Lord in which everything makes sense. We feel a tremendous consolation from the Lord. We experience a sense of unity with God, with others, and even with all of creation. It might be while we are praying or at Mass or Eucharistic adoration or walking along a nature path or when we look at our first grandchild. These moments of insight are called numinous experiences. They tend not to last all that long. The phone rings or the dog barks and we are pulled back into our everyday life. It is like the disciples who climbed up the mountain for the transfiguration but then had to climb down into the valley for their everyday lives. Even though we have to return to our regular activities, we still have the memories of those moments of revelation. It is what keeps us going through the tough times.

We cannot force ourselves to have numinous moments. We can be open to them, but ultimately they are gifts from God which come when God knows it would be best for us.

Questions

1. Should apocalyptic language be interpreted literally?
2. Why did Jesus have such a rough time with the Pharisees?
3. Are there non-Christians today who are more Christian in their actions than I am?
4. Did Jesus multiply the bread and fish once or twice? Why?
5. Do I encounter the glory of God every once in a while (even if just for a moment)? Does it help me get through the difficult times?

Prayer

Jesus, teach me to truly listen to Your teaching and not to only hear what I want to hear. May the Gospel challenge me to convert my whole heart and my whole life to Your love.

Conclusion

THERE is so much more that could be said about the Gospel of Mark. Even though Mark was not the best of authors, he was a good editor. He arranged his material in such a way that it presented a message of its own.

Furthermore, we have to remember that this is eyewitnesses' material. These are the words of Peter and the other Disciples of Christ. The very fact that Mark did not change his material all that much means that we get an accurate picture of what Jesus said and did. This is why reading and studying this Gospel is such a joy, for through it we come to know and appreciate Jesus the Christ, the Son of Man and the Son of God.

Prayer

St. Mark, pray for us.

Part III

The Gospel of Luke

Chapter 1

Luke Writes a Gospel

THERE are legends concerning each of the authors of the four Gospels. Mark is said to be John Mark, a disciple of Peter who had accompanied Paul and Barnabas on one of their missionary journeys. Matthew is said to be the Apostle who was a tax collector when Jesus called him. John is said to be the Beloved Disciple who had a special relationship with Jesus. What do we hear about Luke?

Luke, according to tradition, was a Gentile convert who was a disciple of Paul and a physician. Is this tradition credible?

First of all, let's deal with the question of Luke being a Gentile convert. In both the Gospel which bears his name and in the Acts of the Apostles which he also wrote, there are frequent references to Jewish traditions. Occasionally, however, there are inaccuracies. One example of this is what occurred forty days after the birth of Jesus. We are told that Mary and the baby Jesus were taken to the temple for "their purification." Technically, it was only Mary who had to be purified. This ritual was needed because blood had been spilt during the process of childbirth. There was a different ritual for the child Jesus. He was a first born, and ever since the exodus when God saved the first born of the Israelites, first borns technically belonged to God. They had to be bought back from God with a sacrifice (for the poor, two turtle doves or two pigeons). This was called the rite of redemption. Luke calls what happened forty days after the birth "their" purification, when technically it was Mary's purification and Jesus' redemption. He simply did not know the difference between the two. This fact, that he doesn't know the Jewish traditions all that well, gives credence to the tradition that he was a Gentile Christian.

Even though Luke was not Jewish, he shows great respect for the Jews and Jewish ways. He believed that it was God's plan to call the Jews first, and he therefore treated this plan with respect.

What about the tradition that Luke was one of Paul's disciples? There is a difficulty with this tradition. In the Acts of the

Apostles, Luke occasionally gets details of Paul's story wrong (e.g., compare Luke's version of what Paul did after his conversion to that contained in Galatians). Other times, he does not seem to know what Paul did for rather significant stretches of time (e.g., the fact that Luke only has a couple of stories about Paul's rather extensive mission in Ephesus). If Luke were a Disciple, wouldn't he have known Paul's story better?

There is a way to deal with this difficulty. Throughout most of Acts, Luke tells the story in the third person singular and plural ("he" and "they"). In a few places (16:10ff; 20:5ff; 27:1ff), Luke slips into the first person plural ("we"). It is possible that Luke was a disciple of Paul, but only during the material covered by the "we" sections, which would probably only amount to several months. He was a disciple, but not for all that long.

Finally, was Luke a physician? There are hints in his writings that he was, in fact, a physician. First of all, there is the vocabulary. Luke has a very educated vocabulary. Whenever Luke quotes verses from Mark, he changes a large number of words to more sophisticated words. This is something that one would expect of an educated physician.

A second argument in favor of him being a physician is the fact that Jesus often performs miracles in this Gospel out of compassion. Again, this is something one would expect of a doctor.

The third piece of evidence that Luke is a physician is how he treats a few passages in his Gospel. When Jesus is arrested in the Garden of Gethsemane, one of the Disciples cuts off the ear of the High Priest's slave. Only in the Gospel of Luke do we hear that Jesus put the ear back and healed it. When Jesus heals Simon's mother-in-law, Luke uses a more technical term than is found in the other Gospels to describe her severe fever. Finally, there is the story of the woman who suffered from a hemorrhage for twelve years. In the Gospel of Mark, we hear that the woman had spent all her savings on doctors who didn't do her any good. When Luke tells the same story, he conveniently leaves out the fact that the doctors took all of her money.

For all these reasons, it is very probable that Luke was, in fact, a physician.

Why He Wrote the Gospel

NOW that we know who Luke was, we can ask why and when and where he wrote this Gospel. Mark wrote his Gospel in a simple manner to tell the story of Jesus in a very unsophisticated way for the early Christian community that, according to Paul in First Corinthians, did not include many who were rich or educated. Matthew wrote his Gospel for Jewish Christians who had been expelled from the synagogue. We believe that Luke wrote his Gospel for an educated Gentile audience. His Gospel is much more literary than that of Mark or Matthew. He wrote in good Greek (actually very good Greek).

There is an ancient tradition that he wrote his Gospel in Southern Greece. He wrote it around 80-85 A.D., around the same time that he wrote the Acts of the Apostles and approximately the same time that Matthew was writing his Gospel (although it does not seem that Luke and Matthew knew about each other's Gospels for there are significant differences in their accounts, e.g., the infancy narratives).

What sources did Luke use for his account? We know that he (and Matthew) used the Gospel of Mark. He also used Q, which are those verses that one finds in Matthew and Luke but are not found in Mark. (Some scholars believe that it was Matthew, the tax collector and apostle, who collected the verses contained in Q.) His final source was one which is called "L." This was Luke's own particular material, e.g., that contained in the infancy and resurrection narratives as well as much of the material found from 6:20 to 8:3 and from 9:51 to 18:14. While Mark pasted his sources together as best he could and Matthew constructed an intricate matrix of material from his sources, Luke puts them together with an artistic touch that produces a masterpiece of literature.

A Complicated Prologue

LUKE begins his Gospel with a four-verse-long Prologue in which he sets out why he produced another Gospel. He proposes that it will be an "orderly" account (implying that previous accounts were not quite as orderly).

From the vocabulary that Luke uses in the Prologue, it is obvious that he wants his account not only to be orderly but also educated. Luke uses a number of words in these verses that are so sophisticated that they never again appear in the Bible. He wants to impress his readers. He wanted to make Christianity available to those who were among the better educated in society. This very sophisticated vocabulary was especially important because of the material that follows. The rest of the first two chapters were written in an archaic form of Greek called Septuagint Greek. This was the Greek used in the Greek translation of the Old Testament. It was considered to be simplistic and even a bit crude. If an educated Greek had opened up Luke's Gospel and found the first two chapters of material written in what they would have considered to be poor Greek, chances are that they would never have read further. If, however, Luke begins the Gospel with four verses of highly sophisticated Greek and then continues on in Septuagint Greek, the reader would have known that it was not because the author could not do any better. He would have understood that Luke was writing in Septuagint Greek on purpose.

Finally, Luke dedicates his works (both the Gospel and Acts) to a certain "Theophilus." This might be an important person whose favor Luke was seeking, possibly even someone from the family of the Caesars. We know, for example, that one of the Caesars, a certain Domitilla, converted to Christianity at the end of the first century A.D.

A second possibility was that Theophilus was a rich patron who was going to pay for the transcribing of the Gospel onto scrolls. This was an expensive process and Luke might have needed someone to help him financially.

A third possibility (and the most probable of the three) is that Theophilus is a symbolic name. *"Theos"* in Greek means "God" and "phileo" in Greek means "to love." Theophilus was therefore anyone who loved God, i.e., Christians. Luke might be dedicating his Gospel and the Acts of the Apostles to the early Christian community.

Questions

1. Who was Luke and why did he write his Gospel?
2. Who was Theophilus?

Prayer

God, may I always want to learn more about my faith. May it be a question of both my mind and my heart.

Chapter 2

The Infancy Narratives

A Diptych

THE rest of chapters 1 and 2 are the story of the Annunciation and birth of John the Baptist and Jesus. It is laid out as a diptych, a set of two pictures placed side by side. Each of the pictures has it own value, and together they present a more profound message. John the Baptist's story is miraculous, but that of Jesus is even greater.

As has been said, these chapters are written in Septuagint Greek. Did Luke inherit this account from another source and simply incorporate it into his work without changing it too much, or did he write these chapters this way on purpose? The latter is much more probable, for Luke certainly had no compunctions about changing the Greek in Mark's Gospel. Why would Luke have chosen to use this archaic form of Greek? It is similar to a technique that directors use in films when they want to speak of things that happened long ago. They go from filming in color to filming in black and white. The archaic form of Greek gives that same sense, of events that happened long ago (for they precede the rest of the material in this Gospel by a few decades).

The Annunciation of John the Baptist

THE main part of the Gospel begins with the story of Zechariah going to the temple to perform a sacrifice. (This is why the symbol for this Gospel is an ox, for this is most likely the animal that Zechariah would have sacrificed.)

In those days, there were twenty-four clans of priests, so many that they would only come to the temple to perform sacrifices once every twenty-four weeks. When they arrived, they would cast lots (either pieces of bone or dice) to determine which priest would actually perform the daily sacrifices. This was deemed to be an honor and was also profitable since the priest who performed the sacrifice would receive certain parts of the animal.

Zechariah was chosen, but during the sacrifice he encountered an archangel named Gabriel (one of the three named in the Bible, although in other sources there are another four named). There is no description of what he looked like. Angels do not always appear with wings. Yet, it immediately becomes obvious that Zechariah sensed that something special was going on. The angel tells him that his prayers had been answered and that he and his wife Elizabeth would have a child. Zechariah asked Gabriel how this could be, and Gabriel answered him that because he asked this, he would not be able to speak. Why was Zechariah punished for asking this question while Mary asked the same thing and she was commended? The key to understanding this is found in what Gabriel said, that Zechariah's prayers had been answered. Zechariah and Elizabeth had been praying for a child for a long time, but when Zechariah was told that God would answer those prayers, he didn't believe the power of his own prayers. This is probably why Zechariah was being silenced; he had said enough for the time being. Now he could await the fulfillment of God's promise in silence. Mary, on the other hand, was not praying for a child. The last thing she would have wanted at this point was a child, at least before she was fully married to Joseph.

We hear that Zechariah came home after the time of his service was over and his wife Elizabeth became pregnant. This story is similar to many of the other annunciation stories in the Old Testament. An elderly couple who desperately wanted children were visited by a messenger of the Lord who promised them that they would have a child who would be special to the Lord.

Gabriel Visits Mary

THE same archangel, Gabriel, then visits Mary, a young virgin from Nazareth who is betrothed to Joseph, a carpenter. This is the same description of Mary and Joseph that we find in Matthew with the exception of where Mary and Joseph lived. If one reads Matthew's account carefully, one sees that in his Gospel, Mary and Joseph lived in Bethlehem before the child was born and only moved to Nazareth when they returned from exile in Egypt. Luke has them begin in Nazareth, go to Bethlehem for the birth, and then move back to Nazareth.

Betrothal in those times was a formal contract in which one was considered to be married (although one did not yet live with the betrothed). It was an intermediate time during which one could gather whatever would be needed by the newly married couple.

If Mary was engaged to a carpenter, then she was poor. This was not the best prospect for a marriage in terms of social status. People in these days were carpenters because their families had lost their land in previous generations so they could not be farmers. They were forced to be poorly paid artisans in order to earn a living.

The archangel greets Mary by calling her "full of grace." There is more to this greeting than we see on the surface. In Greek, there is a tense of the verb called the perfect tense. It is used for actions which began in the past but which were still continuing in the present. Mary was already full of grace when the archangel showed up for she was always full of grace from the moment of her conception. This is what we profess when we speak about the dogma of the Immaculate Conception.

This is why Mary could be so available to the invitation of the Lord. Those of us who are damaged by sin often become defensive when we are challenged to do something that seems difficult or even impossible. If someone were to ask us to do a favor, we would likely answer, "What's in it for me?" Mary did not do this. She offered her life and her love to the Lord. She is an example of vulnerability and service.

The Visitation

MARY had just been invited into a mystery of God's love. Her first and continuous response was generosity. Instead of thinking about her own needs, she decided to visit Elizabeth who was six months pregnant and who needed her help.

There is one element to this story that is a bit confusing. Elizabeth is said to be a relative of Mary. Elizabeth was married to Zechariah, a priest. This meant that he and she were both from the tribe of Levi. Mary and Joseph, on the other hand, belonged to the tribe of Judah. In those days, people did not intermarry between tribes. How could Mary and Elizabeth be related? We do not have a clear answer. This is the only Gospel, however, that proposes that John the Baptist and Jesus are related. Mark and Matthew don't say anything about the matter. John, on the other hand, has John the Baptist say that he did not know Jesus. We have to be a bit careful with this statement, however, for it is a little ambiguous. It could mean that John and Jesus were cousins but they had not seen each other for a long time and therefore did not recognize each other, or it could mean that they were cousins but John did not know that Jesus was the Messiah, or it could even mean that they had never met before. We just don't know what John intended to say.

There are some things in scripture that we can't figure out. That doesn't mean that there is something wrong, only that we cannot fully understand it.

Elizabeth greets Mary, telling her that her baby leapt in her womb the moment she heard her greeting. The first person to recognize the presence of Jesus in the world was an unborn child.

Mary expresses her joy and wonder by proclaiming the canticle called "the Magnificat." Much of this hymn is taken from the canticle that Hannah proclaimed when her son Samuel was born (1 Sam 2:1ff).

Are these the exact words that Mary said on this occasion? Most scholars believe that this canticle, that of Zechariah (1:67ff) and that of Simeon (2:29ff) were all likely early Christian hymns. Luke borrowed them because he felt that they well expressed the sentiments of the people involved. This is a common technique in New Testament times, for Paul also quoted pre-existent hymns in 1 Corinthians 13 and Philippians 2.

The Magnificat is a hymn of the *anawim*. The poor in the days of Jesus were despised by those who held power. The rabbis felt that since they were poor, they did not have time to study the law. If they did not study the law, then they did not know the law. If they did not know it, then they did not keep it, and they were therefore sinners. If one met a poor person in the street, one should not even talk to that person lest one be contaminated by that person's sinfulness.

In the Gospel of Luke, we see the exact opposite attitude toward the poor. They are called the *anawim*, the poor ones of God. The *anawim* were the poor, sinners, women, foreigners, etc., anyone who was broken and lived at the margins of society. Because of their brokenness, they were ready to embrace Jesus when He came into their lives because they needed Him (and they knew that they needed Him).

Mary represents the *anawim*, the lowly ones of God. She speaks of the mighty being brought low and the lowly being lifted up. God reverses the fortunes of both the mighty and the powerless.

The Birth of John

LUKE tells us that Mary stayed with Elizabeth for three months and then went home. The way that this is phrased makes it seem as if she left before the child was born. This is strange for one would have expected her to stay around for the birth of the child. There are a few possibilities. Maybe she left because there would be others around at the birth so that she would not be needed; or possibly Luke said this in a clumsy manner and he didn't mean to say that she left before the child was born; or a third possibility was that she had to get home before it was too dangerous for her to travel (for she was already three months pregnant and travel in those days was difficult and often dangerous).

Zechariah and Elizabeth named their child John. In Hebrew, *Johanan* means "Yahweh is merciful." Zechariah then regains his voice and uses it to proclaim God's fidelity to his promises in the canticle called the Benedictus (1:68ff). The central verse, in fact, states that "God has remembered his holy covenant."

The Birth of Jesus

THE story of the birth of Jesus begins with the proclamation of a worldwide census called by Caesar Augustus. This is one detail of the story that is very difficult to sustain. We have many records from the ancient world, but we have no records at all of any worldwide census. There was a census in the province of Judea, but that census occurred in 6 A.D. and not in 6 B.C. when Jesus was probably born. (The monk who invented the modern calendar was named Dennis the Short and he made a small mistake in his calculations.) Furthermore, even if there was a census, one would not have to travel to one's ancestral home; one registered where one was living. Joseph and Mary would have registered in Nazareth if that is where they were living. Finally, the account also mentions that this occurred when Quirinius was the governor of Syria. Quirinius was never really governor of Syria. He was the legate and that occurred in 6 A.D.

What can we say about the census? Matthew had the Holy Family start out in Bethlehem and only move to Nazareth after their exile in Egypt. Luke has them start out in Nazareth and move to Bethlehem, and then move back to Nazareth when the child was born. Luke must not have known exactly what happened, and he used the story of a census that occurred long ago as the way to get the Holy Family from Nazareth to Bethlehem for the birth of the child. In drama, this is called a *"Deus ex machina."*

Even if this detail is not historic, it does offer Luke the opportunity to mention the name Caesar Augustus. By doing this, he is giving an implicit message: that the birth of this child in a back water province would change the great Roman empire. This is later fulfilled when Paul preaches in Rome at the end of the Acts of the Apostles. This is a typical technique used by Luke called foreshadowing. He mentions something, and then we see it fulfilled much later in the text. This is a way of saying that God has a plan which is worked out in God's own time.

We hear that the child was born in a manger because there was no room in the inn. Even if the Holy Family did not travel to Bethlehem to register for the census, they still could have lived in a cave. They were extremely poor. Joseph was, after all, a carpenter which was a sign of extreme poverty. We know that poor people in the Holy Land lived in caves. In Nazareth, for example, everyone lived in caves (which is why Nathanael asked whether anything good could come from Nazareth).

Jesus was clothed in swaddling clothes. These were rags which were wrapped around the baby to keep the child warm.

The Shepherds

LUKE then tells us that the Shepherds were in the fields by night when the angels announced that a savior was born for the people of Israel. Shepherds in the time of Jesus were not well respected. They were considered to be thieves and possibly even murderers. They were representatives of the *anawim*, the broken ones who needed Jesus the most. This is part of a pattern that we see throughout the Gospel of Luke. It begins with Jesus reaching out to the shepherds and ends with Jesus inviting the Good Thief into Paradise. From beginning to end, Jesus reaches out to the *anawim*.

When was Jesus born? We celebrate the birth of Jesus on December 25th, Christmas Day. But if the shepherds were in the fields by night, then Jesus was probably not born in December. Shepherds would stay in the fields during the Spring for that is when the sheep would give birth to their lambs and the shepherds had to be there to help them if they got into trouble during the birthing process.

Why do we celebrate Jesus' birth in December? Early Christians wanted to celebrate this feast on a day that was already a pagan holiday. They didn't want to draw unnecessary attention to themselves, so it was better to celebrate when everyone else was already celebrating something. December 25th was the feast of the birth of the Sun for it is the first day that one could see the day getting longer after the winter solstice. Jesus was the light of the world, so it made sense to take that feast and make it the day to celebrate the birth of Jesus.

The Circumcision and the Presentation

MARY and Joseph had Jesus circumcised on the eighth day. Again, this is typical of Luke's Gospel. The Holy Family (as well as Zechariah and Elizabeth) were observant Jews and salvation came from the Jews. Luke wants us to know that those who were faithful to this tradition would be ready to embrace Jesus when He came into their lives.

Forty days after the birth of Jesus, the Holy Family goes to the temple for Mary's ritual of purification and Jesus' ritual of redemption.

While the Holy Family was in the temple, they encountered Simeon who had been waiting for the Messiah of the Lord. He proclaimed a canticle which speaks of his hopes having been fulfilled. The canticle was probably originally a funeral hymn that Luke borrowed to represent Simeon's sentiments.

Simeon also speaks to Mary and tells her that a sword would pierce her heart. Traditionally, this has been interpreted as referring to the sorrow she would endure when she witnessed the passion of her son. This is the image used on the feast of Our Lady of Sorrows (Sept. 15th). Yet, there is an older interpretation concerning this saying. In the Bible, the heart is where one thinks, not where one feels. When it says that Mary pondered things in her heart, it means that she was trying to figure out what was going on. The sword that would pierce Mary's heart (mind) was the Word of God which was a sword so sharp that it could separate bone from sinew. What revelation would be so profound that it would cut Mary to the quick? It was possibly that her son was the Son of God. She knew very well that her Son was special, that He was the promised Messiah. She knew, after all, how she had gotten pregnant. Yet, in those days, the Messiah was thought of as a hero, not as God Himself. She expected her son to be a king or a general, not God. Furthermore, even if Jesus was called the Son of God, in the Old Testament that term only meant "hero." That is how she would have heard those words. Finally, Mary, being Jewish, prayed every day that there was only one God, Yahweh. How could her son also be God, especially when she was the one who changed His diapers? Of all people who ever lived, she had the hardest time believing that her son was God, and yet she did. How do we know that she believed that Jesus was God? Luke has her present with the early Christian community on Pentecost morning. It was his way of saying that she was the perfect disciple for she believed the Word of God and made it incarnate in the world.

This section closes with the Holy Family encountering Anna, a prophetess who had awaited the consolation of Israel. All throughout the Gospel of Luke, when we hear a story about a man, we also hear a story about a woman.

Jesus Lost in the Temple

THE infancy narrative in Luke ends with one story of Jesus when He was twelve years old. The family went up to Jerusalem for the feast of the Passover. (While this feast was originally a family feast celebrated in one's home, by this time it and Pentecost and the Feast of Booths had become pilgrimage feasts).

Why is this the only story of Jesus from between the time that Jesus was an infant and when He began His public ministry? There must be some reason why Luke would mention this particular episode.

It might be to answer a question: when did Jesus figure out that He was God? Since He was always both God and man, one would think that He always knew it. But Philippians 2 speaks of Jesus surrendering His divine prerogatives, embracing our humanity. Ignorance is part of our human condition. Could Jesus have been one with the Father in love but not know it intellectually? This story might provide the answer. A Jewish boy was considered to be a man at twelve years old. Luke seems to be saying that maybe He knew that He was God when He knew that He was a man. This is, in fact, when He tells His mother that the temple is His Father's house. He recognizes Who His true Father is.

There could also be another level to this story. It might be a foreshadowing, like the mention of the census. Is there another time when Jesus disappears for three days when He is about the Father's business? Isn't that what happened when Jesus died on the Cross? Maybe Jesus was preparing His mother so that when Jesus died and disappeared into the tomb for three days she could still trust.

This could also explain why Jesus did not appear first to His mother on Easter Sunday. One would have expected Him to appear to her first of all, but instead He appears to the Disciples.

Maybe He did not appear to her because she didn't need it; she already trusted.

Questions

1. Why did Luke want to compare the birth of John the Baptist and that of Jesus?
2. Why was Zechariah mute after his encounter with Gabriel?
3. What does "full of grace" mean?
4. What could have been some of the reasons why Mary went to visit Elizabeth? What was the main reason?
5. What is the meaning of the name "John"?
6. What does the fact that Jesus was born in a manger teach us about His mission?
7. Who do the shepherds represent?
8. Why was it important to Luke to show that Mary and Joseph were good Jews?
9. Why does Luke tell us the story of when Jesus was lost in the temple?

Prayer

My Lord Jesus, all of those who witnessed Your birth were filled with joy and a sense of wonder. Please, don't let the difficulties of my life rob me of joy. May I be so joy-filled that all will know that I am one with You by the peace that they find within me.

Chapter 3

The Resurrection Narratives

NOW that we have examined the infancy narrative in the first two chapters of Luke, we will pass to the three stories of the Resurrection contained in chapter 24.

In the first account, the women go to the tomb to anoint the body of Jesus because they had not had enough time to do it on Good Friday. They went to the tomb "very early" in the morning, which meant after one could see light at the horizon but could not yet see the disk of the sun. The account mentions the names of three women who went, and then adds that there were a number of other women with them. Again, this shows the importance of women in this Gospel. In John, there had only been one woman, in Matthew two, in Mark three, but here it seems as if the whole Lady's sodality came out to the tomb.

There are two men dressed in white in the tomb. They are obviously angels, but we have to ask why they are called men and not angels. It has to do with the symbolism of this account. The women hear about the resurrection but they don't see the risen Jesus. This is just like when we first come to the faith. We hear about Jesus from other people, not from angels or directly from a voice from the heavens. The two men represent the fact that we learn about the Resurrection from people (teachers, parents, clergy, etc.)

When the women tell the Disciples what had happened to them, the Disciples consider their tale to be nonsense. This is a bit of a dig at the Disciples. God had chosen the women to be witnesses, why did the Disciples not trust what they were saying?

The second account takes place on the road to Emmaus. The day of the Resurrection, two Disciples set out from Jerusalem to walk to Emmaus. They met a stranger on the way who then accompanied them. It was Jesus, but they did not recognize Him. (There are three times that the Disciples do not recognize Jesus after the Resurrection: here, when Mary Magdalene looked for Jesus in the Garden, and in John 21 when the Disciples were fishing). Other times, they fully recognize Him and are even able to touch the nail marks in His hands and His feet and the wound in His side.

Jesus explains Sacred Scripture to them along the way, and they speak later of their hearts having burned as He spoke. His emphasis here and in the other two Resurrection accounts is that He had to suffer and die just as it had been foretold. This is a Lukan theme: that God had a plan and that it is our duty to follow that plan. When we do, we will find joy (not necessarily happiness). Joy is the sense of peace we find when we are doing what we should, even if it is not all that pleasant at times.

When the Disciples reach the place where they intended to stay for the night, they invited Jesus (Whom they still did not recognize) to stay with them. They began their evening meal and they recognized Jesus in the breaking of the bread. This is obviously a reference to the celebration of the Eucharist. Jesus then disappears from their sight. In this second Resurrection account, the Disciples met Jesus in sacrament and, even if they did not realize it at the time, in Word. This, again, is what we all experience. We first hear about Jesus (as in the first account) and then we meet Him in sacrament and word (as in the second account).

One other detail is worth mentioning. When the Disciples run back to Jerusalem to tell the others what had happened to them, they are told that Jesus had also appeared to Peter. The only way that this would have been possible were if Jesus had appeared to them at the same time that He was appearing to Peter. We call this bilocation. Our resurrected body will not be encumbered by the limitations of time and space. In heaven, we will be with God, our families, our friends, etc., all at the same time. Here on earth, we must choose because we can only be in one place at a time, there we will be with all of them.

The third account has Jesus appearing to the Apostles and commissioning them to preach the forgiveness of sins. They see Jesus face to face. As we continue to grow in faith, we pass from hearing about Jesus from others to meeting Him in sacrament and word until we finally see His presence everywhere (e.g., in worship, in nature, in service to others, etc.). By choosing these particular accounts (of the many from which Luke could have chosen), he gives us a paradigm of the Christian life. This is a wonderful reminder that we pass through stages in our spiritual growth. It is not instantaneous and complete the moment we accept Jesus into our lives. It is a gradual process of discovery and surrender.

Notice how Jesus' Disciples are commissioned to preach the forgiveness of sins. Our faith is supposed to be something that we share with others. A good examination of conscience is to ask what percentage of our parish's budget is spent on evangelizing the unchurched. Most parishes spend most of their money on those who already show up, not on those who are yet to embrace the faith or who have fallen away from it.

The chapter and the Gospel close with a short version of the Ascension. (Luke has a longer version in the Acts of the Apostles.) Jesus ascends into heaven upon the clouds. This is a biblical way of saying that He went into heaven. We know that heaven is not up or down. It is a different dimension of existence where we are one with God. But some Scriptures spoke of the Son of Man coming down from heaven on the clouds, thus Luke speaks of His going back into the clouds. What really happened on Ascension Thursday? We cannot be sure if this is exactly how it happened. If He wanted to, Jesus could have just disappeared from the Disciples' sight. The problem was that if Jesus had done this, the Disciples, who were simple people, might not have understood what was happening. Maybe He did go up into the clouds so that the Disciples could see the fulfillment of Sacred Scripture and understand where He was going.

Question

1. What is the significance of the three separate Resurrection narratives in Luke?

Prayer

Jesus, may I believe what others tell me about You. May I meet You in sacrament and word. May I see Your presence everywhere and at all times.

Chapter 4

Luke's Particular Viewpoint

Parables of Mercy

HAVING looked at the beginning of the Gospel (the Prologue and the infancy narrative) and the end of the Gospel (the Resurrection narrative), both of which are specifically Lukan material, it would be useful to look at some of Luke's parables. While Mark has relatively few parables (mostly on the Word of God) and Matthew's parables deal largely with the coming judgment, Luke's parables speak about mercy and compassion and forgiveness. Some of our favorite parables, in fact, are found only in Luke. Yet, we should read them carefully, for Luke often adds a zinger to his stories that challenges us to see things in an entirely new way.

The story of the Good Samaritan is certainly a good example of this (10:29ff). The Samaritans were a mixture of the poor Jewish people whom the Assyrians had not exiled when they took the educated and richer people off into captivity in 722 B.C. and the pagans whom the Assyrians brought in to replace those exiled. Even though they could be considered to be half-Jews and acknowledged the Torah to be sacred literature, they were considered to be heretics by the Jews. When they volunteered to help the Jewish people rebuild the walls of Jerusalem, their assistance was rejected. They therefore tired to impede the project. John Hyrcanus, one the kings of the Israel, later destroyed the Samaritan temple on top of Mount Gerazim. They hated the Jews and the Jews hated them. Therefore, they would be the last people one would ever consider to be the heroes of a story told to Jewish people.

The parable speaks of a man on a journey from Jerusalem to Jericho. Even today this road is dangerous. It winds through dangerous curves and has hidden caves all along the way. The man was accosted by thieves who left him for dead. A priest and a Levite both passed by and did not stop to help him. Although it is easy to condemn them for their lack of concern, there is actually a good reason why they should not have stopped. First of all, the brigands who had waylaid the man could have been hiding near-by. This was, in fact, one of their techniques. They would use the wounded traveler as a decoy to catch other travelers unawares. This is similar to the fear we experience when we see a car that has broken down at the side of the road. Should we stop and help the person, or are we afraid that it might be a trap?

Furthermore, the priest and Levite were both dedicated to the service of the Lord. If they touched the wounded man, they would have made themselves ritually impure and they would not have been able to participate in the liturgy. They could have asked themselves, "Which is more important, to serve God or man?" For Jesus, the answer to this question was obvious. They should have served the wounded man as the Samaritan man did. The Samaritan not only cared for him on the spot; he also told the innkeeper to charge his account for anything that the man's care might cost. This man was therefore truly his "neighbor's keeper."

The "zinger" in this story is the identity of the man who was charitable. It would be comparable to someone telling a story about the "charitable terrorist." That is so distasteful to us, and yet Jesus purposely chose a hero who was totally unexpected to challenge His listeners to reevaluate their prejudices.

A second parable concerning mercy is that of the barren fig tree (13:6ff). The man in charge of caring for the tree checked with its owner because it wasn't bearing any fruit. The tender was told to dig around it and manure it and give it another chance. This is what God does, He gives us another chance (although we should notice that this was its last chance, for we should not presume upon God's mercy).

In chapter 15, we have two parables in a row that speak about God's attitude toward sinners. The first (15:1ff) speaks of a lost sheep. The shepherd leaves the ninety-nine sheep that are safe to search after the one sheep that was in danger. As we have already seen with the story of the shepherds coming to adore the Christ child and the good thief, God reaches out to those who most need Him. Some people might feel that this is not fair. Why do sinners get more attention from God than those people who remained faithful to Him all along? Shouldn't He show them more love rather than loving the very people who had rejected

Him? The answer is no. God's ways are not fair according to our human standards. God is most of all loving, especially to those who need His love most.

At the end of the story when the lost sheep is found, the shepherd invites his family and friends to a celebration so that they could share in his joy. We are told that God is filled with joy whenever a sinner returns to Him.

The lesson is repeated immediately afterward with the story of the woman who loses a coin (15:8ff) and searches all throughout the house to find it. Again, she celebrates with her neighbors when she finally finds the coin.

This combination of parables that involve a man and then a woman is typical of Luke. The kingdom of God, for example, is like a mustard seed planted in the ground (man's work) and yeast put in dough (woman's work). Both men and women are important in the kingdom.

The message that God only wants sinners to return to Him is reinforced by one of the most famous parables: the Prodigal Son (15:11ff). The story opens with Jesus speaking of a man who had two sons. The younger son goes to his father and asks him for his inheritance. This is not only presumption. It is also thoughtlessly cruel, for he is effectively telling his father that he wished that he were dead.

The son takes his inheritance and squanders it on loose living. When he has gone through his money, those whom he thought were his friends abandoned him. He ends up feeding pigs (Remember the horror that this detail would evoke in a Jewish audience). He realizes that his father's servants had more than enough to eat while he was starving, so he decided to return to his father and beg him for forgiveness.

It is not clear whether the son's apology is sincere. Is he truly sorry for what he did, or is he only saying what is necessary to get back into his father's favor?

It is the father's reaction that is astounding. If he were a good Jewish father, then he would have had his son put to death (for this was the law of Israel). If he had not done this, then he should at least have waited in his house until his son came on his hands and knees and begged for his forgiveness. Instead, the father waited outside for his son and ran to him when he caught sight of him.

Notice that the father forgives his son even before he got a chance to ask for that forgiveness. Maybe he did this because he knew that the son's apology was only a line. He even ordered that a feast be prepared to celebrate his son's return.

The young man's older brother then arrived. He was furious that his father would forgive his good-for-nothing brother. He was angry that his father would seem to treat the brother better than he had treated him even though he had stayed and worked for his father the whole time. The father begged his older son to celebrate with him for, as he said, "your brother was dead and now he is alive."

There are so many lessons we can learn from this parable. First of all, it speaks of God's mercy and how He desires that we turn from our sin and live. It also speaks of God's great respect for our freedom (He let the younger son go on his way even though He knew it could be disastrous). God does not force us to love Him; He invites us.

We should also hear that we don't earn God's forgiveness. It is based upon the fact that the other person needs it, not that the person deserves it. We realize that what the person did was a symptom of his/her brokenness. All that we want is to love that person into healing.

We can also learn from the older brother's reaction (which, if we are honest, is similar to our own attitude at times). If God was just according to our standards, He would have rewarded the older brother and shunned the younger brother. Instead, He was more concerned with mercy than justice.

Finally, we should notice what the father says to the older son. Everything the father had was always his. The reward for doing good deeds is to be able to do those good deeds. Heaven is not only what we will receive at the end of time. It already begins now. We are already in heaven inasmuch as we are living in love. If the only reason why we do good is to obtain an eternity of pleasure in heaven, aren't we being a bit selfish? Isn't heaven where we will be like God, and God reveals Himself as one Who reaches out to us in mercy and service and love?

The next parable does not concern God's mercy as much as the call to show compassion to those around us (similar to the story of the Good Samaritan). It is the story of the rich man and Lazarus (16:18ff). This is not Lazarus, the brother of Mary and Martha. Lazarus was a rather common name in New Testament times. This was simply a terribly poor man.

There was a rich man who refused to help poor Lazarus. The rich man is sometimes called "Dives," which is the Latin word for "rich man." When he dies, he is sent to hell as a punishment for not helping Lazarus while he was alive. Lazarus goes to heaven where he is in the bosom of Abraham. (The image being presented is that of the heavenly banquet. In ancient times, people reclined at table. Lazarus was given the seat next to Moses and could lean back onto his chest like the Beloved Disciple did to Jesus at the Last Supper).

The rich man's punishment is a reminder that we will be judged on the basis of how we have treated our brothers and sisters (the same message as found in the parable of the separation of the sheep from the goats).

God also refuses to send more warnings to the rich man's brothers. He tells the rich man that they already have received enough messages. God cannot force us to convert, He can only invite us. We should never claim that we didn't know what we were supposed to do for we have already been warned.

Another parable that combines the ideas of mercy and judgment is that of the Pharisee and the publican (18:9ff). The Pharisee was full of himself. He bragged about his religious practices as if that earned him special consideration. The publican, on the other hand, humbly admitted his guilt. The humble publican was forgiven while the Pharisee was not (for he was self-righteous). God offers His mercy, but we have to be willing to reach out for it. If we think that God owes us something, then we can never really become vulnerable. It is only when we recognize our brokenness and our need for forgiveness that we can open our hearts to the love that God is offering us all the time.

The final story is not a parable but it is a continuation of the theme we have been studying: that of Zaccheus (19:1ff). Jesus entered the city of Jericho where a certain Zaccheus lived. He was a tax collector. People hated tax collectors. No one likes to pay taxes, but beyond this there was the fact that tax collectors were considered to be collaborators with the occupying power: Rome. Furthermore, the system of tax collection in those days was inherently dishonest. Someone would put out a bid for the right to collect the taxes in a certain area. He would pay up front, and then everything he collected would belong to him. The people living there had few legal rights, so he could bully the people to give him whatever he wanted.

We also hear that Zaccheus was short, but he desperately wanted to see Jesus, so he climbed up a Sycamore tree. One can picture how absurd it would have appeared to the people standing nearby. The children were probably standing by and throwing stones at him (while the parents silently approved).

Jesus called Zaccheus down and speaks to him, inviting Himself to supper. The people were annoyed. Why on earth would Jesus go to this sinner's house? But it was exactly because the man was a sinner that He went to his house. Zaccheus is an *anawim*, someone who needed His love and healing.

Zaccheus responds to this kindness by promising to repay many times over anyone he might have defrauded (which was very possible considering he was a tax collector). Jesus is very pleased and He tells Zaccheus that "today salvation" was coming to his house.

First of all, notice that salvation was coming "today." In theology, there are two types of eschatology (the teachings concerning what will happen at the end of time). There is future eschatology which says that these things will be fulfilled at some future date. But there is also present eschatology which speaks about the promises being fulfilled now. What sort of salvation is occurring now? As soon as we meet Jesus, we are already saved from fear and hate and sin. We are already experiencing heaven here on earth.

Luke also presents this idea by his use of certain terms concerning healing. Whenever Jesus heals someone and there is no expression of faith, Luke simply says that the person was "healed." When there is an expression of faith, then Luke uses the word "saved" to describe what happened to the person. The person was not only healed physically; that person was healed spiritually as well.

Prayer and God's Will

NOW that we have looked at these parables and stories, we can address certain themes that are found throughout the Gospel. The first we will look at is prayer. In the Gospels of Mark and Matthew, Jesus prays relatively few times: twice and three times respectively. In Luke, He prays eleven. That is quite a considerable change, and it obviously means something.

In Luke, Jesus prays whenever He is about to do something important, e.g., when He chooses the Apostles (6:12fff), when He asks Peter who people think that He is (9:18), when He is transfigured (9:28), etc. He prays in order to discern the Father's will for Him and to be able to fulfill it. God has a plan for each one of us and we will only find joy if we cooperate with that plan. Luke develops the idea of God having a plan in a number of ways. We have already seen that he mentions one idea in a passage and then has it fulfilled later in the text. He also uses the word "must" frequently. Furthermore, he speaks of kings and then applies that title to God. This shows that God is in charge, but to make sure that God does not come across as an autocrat, he balances this term with the word "father." This shows us that God is a loving parent Who only wants what is good for us.

This brings up the ideas of obedience and discipline. In modern America, these almost sound like dirty words, but in the Bible they are words that designate surrender to God's will. This is how we can become the best person that we could ever be.

Luke does not go into the question of how specific God's will is (e.g., Does God have a specific vocation for each one of us? Does God meddle in day-to-day questions of what we are going to eat or wear? etc.); or how God's will interacts with free will. (A healthy image of the interaction of God's will and free will might be that of a partnership in which God is the senior partner.) Nor does he give a guideline of how to discern the Father's will other than to pray (e.g., One could also speak of spiritual reading, fasting, spiritual direction, looking for signs, taking baby steps in our actions, trying to find peace with our decisions, etc.)

Intercessory Prayer

THERE is also another purpose for prayer in Luke (17:1ff; 18:1ff) which is to ask for those things which we need. If one were to ask a room full of Christians, "Do we change God's mind when we pray?" the most frequent answer would probably be, "No!" If we were to press on and ask those people why we pray, then people would most likely say, "To learn to accept what God was going to send anyway." This is a wonderful spiritual thought, but it is just not what Jesus teaches in Luke's Gospel. He speaks of a persistent widow who nags an evil judge into giving her her rights (18:1ff). The judge eventually gives in just to get her off his back. The remarkable thing about this parable is that the evil judge represents God the Father. The lesson is that prayer changes reality.

Again, Luke does not explain how it changes reality. To give a simple explanation, we could say that when we pray for someone, our love joins God's love and that love visits the person for whom we are praying. When people are loved, it changes their reality. There was an experiment done in an infirmary in which some babies were held and caressed; others were not. The babies who were caressed thrived; the ones that were not did not thrive. Prayer is a spiritual caress. Even if the person does not know that we are praying for him/her, the person can sense it for there is a level of communication that goes beyond words (like when one thinks about a friend and the phone rings and the friend is on the line). One caution is necessary, though, for at times God's answer to our prayers is "no" for that is the most loving answer God can give us. Whether God says "no" or "yes," it will be because that is the most loving answer that God could possibly give us in the situation in which we find ourselves.

Prayer is one of the most important and powerful things that we can do. God created the world with words, and we help recreate it in His image when we pray.

Jerusalem

IN Mark and Matthew, most of the action takes place in Galilee. Jesus only goes up to Jerusalem at the end of the Gospel. In Luke and John, Jerusalem is much more important. Luke considers Jerusalem to be the chosen city in which God's plan for salvation will be revealed. This is why we hear about Jerusalem and the temple so early in the story (i.e., the account of Zechariah's annunciation, the presentation in the temple, the story of Jesus being lost in the temple). Then, in 9:51, Jesus heads for Jerusalem. From that moment on, He is heading to His destiny, even if it is not until 19:28 that He actually arrives in Jerusalem.

Then in the Acts of the Apostles, we see that the Good News goes forth from Jerusalem, the religious center of the universe, to Rome, the political center of the universe.

This theme reinforces the idea that God has a plan, but also that there are special places, holy places, where we can encounter the Holy One. God is everywhere, but there are certain places that help us to be receptive to His presence. This is the idea behind shrines and pilgrimages.

Kings

WE have already seen that Luke uses the term "king" for God. This title reminds us that God is in charge of our lives.

But it seems as if there is another reason for his use of the title king and his naming of kings and governors. He is possibly trying to write a bit of an apologia for his community, i.e., telling the Roman authorities that Christians are good citizens and at the same time reminding Christians to be good citizens. This is exactly what a Jewish general, Flavius Josephus, did after he was captured by the Romans during the Jewish Civil War. He wrote a history of the Jewish people to show the Romans that the Jews were not really bad people. They only had been misled by the Zealots.

Likewise, Luke gives an apologia for his own Christian community. Was it an attempt to convince the Romans not to persecute Christians (something that they had already begun to do)?

Was the reticence of Pilate to kill Jesus (23:1) and of Gallio to punish Paul (Acts 18:12) a signal to Roman authorities that this is the way that they should really act?

Jesus Brings Peace

BEING a stoic, Luke longed for a well-ordered community in which people lived in peace. He considered it to be essential for the Christian community to give a good example. When Jesus came into our lives, it was supposed to change everything.

This is why Luke speaks of the idealistic life of the early Christian community in Acts 2:42ff and 4:32ff. Luke also shows how even during the life of Jesus, people got along when He came into their lives. Pilate sent Jesus to Herod (Lk 23:6ff). Before this time, Pilate and Herod had hated each other, but after Jesus comes into their lives, they become the best of friends.

Luke is a bit of a Pollyanna in his descriptions. Even he has to admit that there were disagreements, but he also strongly emphasizes the good will of the community. Might his descriptions of community life be less of a description of how the community actually was and more of a goal toward which the community should aim?

Food

IT is interesting how many times Luke mentions food in his Gospel. Parables often revolve around meals, e.g., the father of the prodigal son celebrates his return with a meal; the rich man is punished for not sharing his meal with Lazarus, etc. Jesus gives His most important instructions at the Last Supper. He even eats fish when He rises from the dead. Heaven is even described as a heavenly banquet.

This is very odd because Stoics did not believe in enjoying food. The good Stoic, in fact, was the one who fasted until he died for as he wasted away, he became less and less material (which they considered to be evil) and more and more spiritual. This is one area in which Luke rejected his Stoic roots when he became a Christian. He affirmed the goodness of this world and all of its creatures.

Questions

1. How can we reconcile the compassionate message of this Gospel with the Old Testament presentation of God?
2. What do I do to discern God's will for me?
3. When I pray, do I change God's mind?
4. Are there special places where it is easier for me to pray and to experience God's presence?
5. Is God the king of my life?
6. What does "peace" and "joy" mean to me?
7. Are my meals sacred moments for me to be present with God and those around me?

Prayer

Loving Jesus, open my heart to Your compassion. May I experience Your love and mercy in a powerful way, and may I share Your compassion with those who most need it.

Chapter 5

The Beginning of the Ministry

John the Baptist

NOW that we have examined various large narrative sections and themes, we can look at some short passages. Some of these stories were borrowed from Mark or Q which Luke then changed to push his own agenda. At other times they are stories found only in Luke. It might be useful to follow along in the Gospel so that one can better see the points being made in this treatment.

The passage that speaks about the preaching of John the Baptist begins with the names of a number of civil and religious officials (remember how Luke liked to be a name dropper to show that Christians were good citizens). What is very unusual in Luke's account is how John gives advice to tax collectors and soldiers. Normally, Jewish authorities wouldn't have anything to do with either of these, but John the Baptist does not condemn them. He does not order them to leave their occupations, jobs that many considered to be corrupt and tainted with collaboration tendencies. Rather, he simply told them to do their jobs as well as they could. That would be enough for them to be considered to be righteous.

This was also a message for Luke's community. He was telling them that they could participate in many different occupations and still be good people as long as they did those jobs with the proper spirit.

The Genealogy of Jesus

IN 3:23ff, we hear the genealogy of Jesus. It is different from the list found in Mt 1:1ff. While Matthew traced Jesus' ancestry to Abraham and David, Luke traces His ancestry all the way back to Adam. Jesus had not only come to save the Jewish people. He had come to save all humankind.

One should not try to reconcile these two lists. These genealogies were more symbolic than historic. It is not that one list is right and the other not. Both are true in their symbolism.

The Temptations in the Desert

L IKE the Gospel of Matthew, Luke speaks of three temptations in the desert (4:1ff). The devil tried to entice Jesus to
misuse His authority for selfish purposes. In Matthew, mountains were very important. They were where one experienced
God's revelation. The last temptation, therefore, occurs on a
mountain. In Luke, the importance of Jerusalem is emphasized.
This is why the last temptation occurs on the parapet of the temple in Jerusalem (4:9ff).

The Spirit of the Lord

I N Matthew, Jesus goes into the synagogue in Nazareth after He
performed various miracles that showed that He had the
power to do anything: a nature miracle (Mk 4:35), an exorcism
(Mk 5:1ff), and a healing (Mk 5:21ff).

In this Gospel, He visits the synagogue as His first act of His
public ministry. He quotes a proclamation from the Book of the
Prophet Isaiah to define His ministry.

Jesus describes His ministry as proclaiming the Good News
to the poor and liberty to captives. He was to initiate a year
acceptable to the Lord. Normally, the promises contained in this
passage were fulfilled when the Jewish people celebrated their
Sabbatical and Jubilee years. Slaves were set free; debts were
forgiven; land was returned to its original owner. Jesus was proclaiming Himself to be the embodiment of these celebrations.
One would no longer have to wait for seven years or even for
fifty years for these things to happen. When Jesus came into the
world, He established a new order of mercy and compassion. He
called us all to live as brothers and sisters, sharing what is in
excess to feed the poor (Remember the description of the early
Christian community in Acts 2 and 4).

As in Mark, Jesus is rejected by His own (although Luke softens Jesus' words so that He does not include His own family
among those who reject Him). Jesus then speaks of foreigners in
the history of Israel who were favored by the Lord: the widow of
Zarephath and Namaan the Syrian. If the Jews rejected Jesus,

then He would reach out to the Gentiles. This is part of Luke's message: first the Jews and then the Gentiles.

Questions

1. How can I make my work holy to the Lord?
2. Who is invited to Christ's banquet?
3. What are the most common sources of temptation in my life? How do I fight against these temptations?
4. Now that Jesus is part of my life, do I live each day as if it were a spirit-filled day?

Prayer

Holy Spirit of God, guide me and consecrate me in Your truth and love. Inspire me with Your Spirit and send me into the world to proclaim Your Good News.

Chapter 6

Jesus' Mission of Compassion

The Beatitudes

THE Beatitudes are found in the Gospels of Matthew and Luke. This means that they were originally part of the Q source, those sayings that appear in Matthew and Luke and do not appear in Mark. In Matthew, they are part of the Sermon on the Mount. This is typical of Matthew's Gospel where important revelations occur on mountains. In Luke, the Beatitudes are presented on the plain (which is probably more historic).

In Matthew, there are eight positive Beatitudes while in Luke there are four positive and four negative Beatitudes. The latter is a more Jewish way of teaching. This is how Joshua renewed the covenant with God when the Israelites entered the promised land. He had one group of priests stand on one mountain and another on the opposite mountain. One group would shout out, "Blessed are those who honor their parents, etc.," while the other groups shouted out, "Cursed are those who do not." Since Luke contains both blessings and curses, his version is probably closer to what Jesus actually said than Matthew's version.

The other major difference between Matthew and Luke is that Matthew's version of the Beatitudes is more spiritualized (e.g., blessed are the poor in spirit, blessed are those who hunger and thirst for righteousness) while Luke's version is more physical (blessed are those who are poor, blessed are those who hunger and thirst). This fits Luke's belief that the *anawim* are most able to embrace Jesus' message because they are not trapped by their riches. They live in need and they know that they are in need, and so when someone comes along who answers that need, they are ready to accept Him.

The next section continues the themes of loving one's neighbor and praying for those who persecute one (the same material as that found in Mt 5:38ff). There are a few subtle changes. Instead of saying, "The pagans do the same," Luke speaks of "the sinners." This makes sense if Luke is writing for Gentiles and Gentile Christians. He does not want to insult them by using them as an example of those without virtue. Luke also adds the idea of lending money to those who might not repay the debt. Then, whereas Matthew speaks of being perfect as our heavenly Father is perfect, Luke speaks of being merciful as our heavenly Father is merciful (showing again the difference between a converted Pharisee who was concerned with righteousness and a converted physician who was concerned with mercy and compassion).

The Widow of Naim

ONE of the miracles that appears only in Luke is the story of the raising of the son of the widow of Naim (7:11ff). Typical of Luke's Gospel, Jesus performs this miracle out of compassion. The widow had been left all alone in the world. The only Jewish institution which would help her was gleaning, the gathering of those crops that the harvesters had missed. Jesus performed the miracle of raising her son for her benefit.

This is not the case of a resurrection of the dead, however, for it is a reanimation. In a resurrection, one receives a new body that no longer suffers from the limitations of this human body. One will never die again. With reanimation, one comes back to life with this present physical body so one would one day have to die again.

The Anointing of the Feet of Jesus

THERE is an anointing story in all four Gospels, but the details vary considerably between the Synoptic version and that found in John. In John it is Mary, the sister of Martha and Lazarus, who anoints the feet of Jesus. In Matthew, Mark and Luke, an unnamed woman anoints the feet of Jesus as an act of courtesy. It is only in Luke that we hear that the woman anointing the feet of Jesus was a great sinner. In this account, the people object not because of the extravagance of her action but because she was unclean. The Pharisee who invited Jesus even objects that if this man were really a prophet, then He would have known what type of woman she was and He wouldn't have let her touch Him.

But it is exactly because Jesus knows that she is a sinner that He treats her with such kindness. She needs Him, and He responds with compassion. This is still another example of Jesus reaching out to the *anawim*, the poor ones of God. Jesus tells His host that her great love brought her great forgiveness.

The Women Who Serve Jesus

IN Lk 6:12ff, we hear about the call of the twelve Apostles. It is important in Luke that there be twelve of them. This was part of God's plan. This is why in Luke Judas must be replaced by another Apostle (Matthias) at the beginning of the Acts of the Apostles. Paul gives a different definition of what it means to be an Apostle. He speaks of Apostles as anyone who gives witness to the risen Jesus. He considered himself to be as good an Apostle as the others.

In 8:1ff, Luke balances out the call of these male Apostles with the report of the women who followed Jesus and served their needs. Luke often balances a story of a man or men with a woman or women, e.g., baby Jesus brought to Simeon and also to Anna. In the other Gospels, the women are not mentioned by name until the Passion. Here, they are His disciples even during His public ministry.

The Transfiguration

ALL three Synoptic Gospels report the Transfiguration, but typically each has slightly different details in each of their versions. Luke, for example, is the only one that specifically mentions that Jesus went up the mountain with Peter, James and John to pray, consistent with Luke's emphasis upon prayer. Then, a couple of times in the account, Luke speaks of Moses and Elijah as "the two men," reminiscent of the two men who gave witness to the Resurrection on Easter morning. Luke also emphasizes the transcendent nature of the event by speaking about how the Disciples were heavy with sleep. (Remember how a number of Old Testament figures received their revelations from God in either sleep or a trance.) Still, although the Disciples were afraid, they enter the cloud that overshadows them. This sounds like an invitation for those reading the Gospel to take heart and enter the mystery of God.

Jesus Is Rejected by the Samaritans

IN 9:52ff, we hear that Jesus passed through Samaria on His way to Jerusalem (a journey which began in the previous verse). The Samaritans would not welcome Him because He was headed to Jerusalem. The disciples, in a fit of self-righteous indignation, asked Jesus to cause fire to come down from the skies upon their village. Jesus rebukes them, for He has come for everyone and not just for the Jews.

Questions

1. How are Luke's Beatitudes different from those found in Matthew?
2. Why did Jesus raise the son of the widow of Naim?
3. Do we love because our sins are forgiven, or are our sins forgiven because we love?
4. Why does Luke emphasize the role of women in his Gospel?
5. Why are Moses and Elijah present at the Transfiguration?
6. Does Jesus respond to the Samaritans' rejection with anger or compassion?

Prayer

God, help me to see my own brokenness and how much I need You. May Your love heal that brokenness so that my love for You may grow ever more sincere.

Chapter 7

Jesus on His Way to Jerusalem

The Mission of the Seventy

THIS is the only Gospel that mentions that in addition to the twelve Apostles, there was another group of disciples, the "seventy" (10:1ff) whom Jesus sent out on mission. This number is probably an allusion to the seventy elders whom Moses chose to share in his authority. They return rejoicing that they were able to exercise power over demons. Jesus acknowledges this, but then tells them that the greater honor is that their names were written in heaven. In the enthusiasm of their first mission, the seventy had focused on their power and not on the deeper meaning of their ministry, that it revealed a relationship of love with God. When we preach the Word of God, whether it be in a formal ministry or simply by giving good example in one's own family, it is easy to become self-righteous and to focus on the negative as opposed to celebrating God's love and mercy. We can become so focused on the wrong things happening around us that we forget to see the good things that are also occurring in our midst.

Martha and Mary

THIS is also the only Gospel that speaks of the episode in which Martha complains because her sister Mary is not helping her with the housework associated with entertaining their guests (10:38ff). Jesus tells Martha that Mary had chosen the better portion by spending time with Him while Martha was running around doing things. Can you see how this is a parallel to the story of the seventy returning, that like Martha they had gotten caught up with what they were doing (exorcising demons) and not on what it meant (having a relationship with God)?

Throughout much of the history of the Church, this passage has been used to argue that the contemplative life is better than the active life. Since the Second Vatican Council, the Church has stated that each form of life is good if that is what God has called us to do.

One can also apply this story to family life. We sometimes get so caught up with doing things (e.g., the preparation for Christmas, a big family meal) that we all but ignore the people around us. One example is that we sometimes work ourselves to death to buy a house for our family, but then we don't have quality time to spend with them. The moral of this story is just as valid today as it always was.

The Our Father

LIKE the Beatitudes, the Our Father comes from the source that we call Q, those sayings that are in Matthew and Luke but which are not found in Mark. Typically, Luke begins his version by telling us that Jesus was praying just before His Disciples asked Him to teach them to pray. Like the Beatitudes too, Luke probably has the more original version. In Luke, the Our Father is simply a series of petitions banded together; in Matthew it is a formally developed prayer. Luke probably is telling us what Jesus actually said while Matthew gives the Our Father that was in use in the community when Matthew was writing his Gospel.

The line in the Our Father that bothers many people is "Lead us not into temptation," as if God would try to tempt us to sin. A better translation of this verse would probably be, "Deliver us from the trial." There was a belief that at the end of the world there would be a period of tribulation in which everyone's faith would be tested and purified. The person praying this verse recognized that he/she was not sure of his/her faith and whether that faith was strong enough to lead one through the difficult times that were coming. The person asks to be protected and strengthened during that time of trial (whether it be the trial and tribulation at the end of times or the everyday trials that we face in living our faith).

True Blessedness

THIS is also the only Gospel that contains the story of a woman who proclaims, "Blessed is the womb that bore You..." (11:27f). Jesus responds, "Blessed rather are those who hear the Word of God and keep it." Jesus is not excluding His mother from the category of the blessed when He says this. In the Gospel of Luke, Mary is the perfect disciple. She is the one who listens to God's invitation to be the mother of her Son and accedes to it. Luke consistently softens those sayings from Mark which would imply that the family of Jesus had a difficult time accepting Him as the Messiah. Jesus is saying that her blessedness is not due to biological considerations. It is due to the depth of her faith.

The Danger of Riches

WE have already heard how the Gospel of Luke shows a preference for the *anawim*, the poor ones of God, for they are those who are most ready to embrace Jesus and His message. At the same time, there is a warning for those who are rich because they could easily think themselves self-sufficient and spend all their energy on accumulating riches.

We hear this when Jesus addresses the question of an inheritance (12:13ff). How often inheritances give rise to family disputes! Jesus argues that it is just not worth it.

We see this theme again when Jesus speaks about the man who tore down his barn to build a bigger one (12:16ff). The man was going to die that very night and his possessions would belong to someone else. Our possessions cannot bring us true security and peace. They are, in fact, more likely than not to get us into trouble for they cause us to be too self-sufficient. (James speaks of this in his letter when he states that our every plan should be conditioned with the phrase, "if God wills it."

Luke speaks of it again in sayings taken from Q in which he speaks about the birds of the air and the lilies of the field and how our treasures should be in heaven (12:22ff). All of these episodes provide a powerful call to put in proper perspective the importance of the things of this world.

What would Jesus say about a middle class life style? What is the balance between prudent preparations for retirement and selfish concern with one's own comfort? What does simplicity (in dress, recreation, food, housing) have to do with the kingdom of God? How do we know if we have too much? These are all questions that we must reflect upon.

A Pair of Miracles

IN 13:10ff and 14:1ff, there are a pair of miracles on the Sabbath. Typical of Luke, the first involves a woman and the second involves a man. The woman is healed from a stooped condition (possibly caused by the bending of the spine that we recognize as a result of osteoporosis) while the man is healed from dropsy (a rampant form of edema caused by liver problems). Jesus is confronted by Pharisees who object to His working on the Sabbath. Their point is that these people had been ill for a long time. What would the problem have been with waiting for another day? Jesus' point is that they have been waiting for a long time and He wouldn't make them wait for another minute. He justifies His action by citing exceptions to the work law on the Sabbath (e.g., feeding one's ox, rescuing a child who had fallen into a wall). These two episodes remind us that the Sabbath is for worship and rest but also for doing good (e.g., visiting a nursing home, inviting a lonely relative to supper at our house, etc.).

Supper Stories

A SERIES of supper stories and sayings follow (14:3ff) reminding us how important food is for Luke.

The first is found only in Luke and it suggests that when one goes to a banquet, one should choose the less important seat lest someone more important arrive and one be asked to move to a lesser seat. It is a question of whether one only seeks recognition and prestige in what one does (e.g., volunteering for a charity, at work, in one's family relations) or whether one seeks to be humble.

Ironically, the one command of Jesus that most Catholics always observe is to seat themselves in the last seat in the Church. It is almost as if we are saying by where we sit that we really don't want to be there and we want to get it over with as soon as possible.

A second dinner saying is that when we have a banquet, we should invite those who can't pay us back. This could be applied to whom we invite to Christmas and Easter meals (even inviting the difficult relatives whom no one else wants around) or those with whom we associate at those meals (choosing to spend time with those who are lonely as opposed to those with whom we have a good time).

The third supper passage is the parable of the great supper which comes from Q. It is the parable of the king (Mt) or rich man (Lk) who throws a banquet and invites guests who do not come. He therefore invites others to the banquet so that it might be filled. The only major difference is that Luke does not include the information about the one man who comes without a wedding garment and who is therefore punished. We have to ask whether this was an addition in Matthew's Gospel, possibly another saying that he had from his sources. Maybe he didn't know where to put this saying, and so he stuck it on to the end of this story because both involved weddings. That would explain why in Matthew's version (Mt 22:1ff), it seems a bit unfair. How could the man be expected to have a wedding garment when he was pulled off the street? Once again, Luke probably has the more original version.

Counting the Cost

IN 14:25ff, Luke expands the saying concerning the cost of discipleship. He speaks of choosing Jesus over our family and taking up one's cross to follow Him. (Although in Luke, there is a very Jewish formulation for Luke has Jesus say that we must "hate" one's family, a Jewish way of saying that we must love Jesus more than one's own family.) But Luke goes on to speak of counting the cost of one's commitment before one makes one's choices (e.g., making sure that one has enough funds to complete a construction project or enough troops to fight a battle). To be a disciple is not easy, and one has to be willing to pay the price. Sitting on the fence and hedging one's bets is not enough; one has to surrender totally to God's will and love.

The Wicked Steward

THERE is a most unusual parable in Lk 16:1ff. Jesus speaks of a steward who is called to task for cheating on his duties. He was fired, but before he left, he decided to make friends for himself with the people who owed his master grain and oil, etc. It almost sounds as if Jesus is condoning dishonesty. Part of the explanation could be that the amounts were exaggerated because he had been charging the debtors unfair interest. Yet, that is not really the point that Jesus was making. He is speaking about cleverness. In the Middle East, being clever, knowing how to get things done, was considered to be an important virtue. In the West, we might consider this to be sneaky, but in the East it was regarded as creative and resourceful.

Jesus' point is that we tend to be clever in affairs of the world. Why is it that we can be so slow in things of heaven? For example, we can figure out how to see our favorite TV program if we will be away from home (even if that means we have to call the grandkids to program our VCR or TiVo), but sometimes we cannot find enough time to pray. We can figure out what to say to get back at someone for a slight, but we cannot figure out how to make peace with that same person. If the Kingdom of God is really that important to us, then we should use all of our resources to secure it.

What Thanks Should We Expect?

LUKE has a very challenging saying in 17:7ff. He asks what gratitude a servant should expect for having done his duty. Sometimes when we try to follow God's law, we feel that God owes us. We are good; therefore God should give us a good biopsy, winning lottery numbers, a trouble free life, etc. But wasn't being good what we wanted to do all along, or were we just good in the hope of obtaining a great reward?

Even when we talk about heaven, it sometimes sounds as if we are just following God's law to earn an eternity of pleasure. Isn't that selfish, only thinking of our own profit (even if it is in terms of eternity)? What if in heaven we will continue to work and serve (although it will not be frustrating as it often is here on earth)? What if our reward will be the opportunity to continue to do what we are already doing here?

Gratitude

THE other side of the coin is the willingness to be grateful for all that God has done for us. Jesus heals ten lepers (17:11ff), but only one returns to thank Him and that was a Samaritan. This provides two of Luke's themes: gratitude and the fact that the hero of the story is an *anawim*, a foreigner.

People sometimes feel as if they have worked hard to earn everything they have. Why should they be grateful? They fail to recognize that they could have been born without many of their talents or they could have been born in a country where even with those talents they would not have had the opportunity to earn enough to feed their own family. We have been so blessed.

Furthermore, we often ask God or the saints for a favor. Do we remember to thank them when we receive a response to our prayers, even if it is not necessarily the response that we wanted? If a friend only called us when that person needed a favor, how long would that person remain a friend?

Questions

1. What is the true source of joy for one who follows Jesus?
2. Am I more of a Martha or a Mary?
3. Do I rely on set prayers or do I simply say what I am feeling?
4. Do I consider myself to be blessed, and if so, why?
5. Do I let what I possess become too important to me?
6. Why is food so important to Luke?
7. Am I as clever in things of faith as I am in the concerns of everyday life?
8. Do I expect God to give me a great reward (here or in heaven), or am I simply pleased to be able to follow Him?

Prayer

Thank You, Lord, for Your presence in my life. Thank You for my faith, my family, the ways that You have blessed me, and even for the crosses which You have asked me to carry in Your name.

Chapter 8

The Last Days of the Life of Jesus

Jesus Weeps Over Jerusalem

A FTER Jesus entered Jerusalem on Palm Sunday, He lamented the pain that the city would see (19:41ff). Unlike Matthew who almost revels in the destruction that would come upon his persecutors, Luke reports that Jesus felt compassion. God does not desire the death of sinners, but that they turn from sin and live. For Luke, Jerusalem was the focal point of God's revelation. How could Jesus desire its ruin?

The Last Supper

T HERE are slight differences in Luke's account of the Last Supper (22:15ff). He speaks of the Passover being fulfilled in the kingdom. It seems as if he is referring to the Last Supper meal being fulfilled on the cross.

Jesus also speaks of His blood being poured out for many. Instead of saying that the cup contains Jesus' blood as we hear in Matthew and Mark however, Luke says that the cup contains the covenant in Jesus' blood, a version that is also found in Paul's First Letter to the Corinthians. This might have been a softening of Jesus' words because the original phrasing, that the cup contained blood, might have been too disturbing for Gentiles. This is one case where Matthew's and Mark's version might be more original, but this also shows us a bit of a connection between Luke and Paul (that they use the same phrasing).

Last Minute Instructions

B ECAUSE meals were so important to Luke, it should not surprise us that Jesus gives some of His most important teachings, a type of last testament, at the Last Supper. In the ancient world, in fact, these last instructions were believed to carry special importance for they encapsulated all of what the person had tried to say throughout his life.

Jesus first tells His Apostles that they should not exercise their authority as the pagans did. They were to measure their importance on how much they served others, and not on how much they were served.

Jesus speaks of how Satan would sift them out like wheat. He then turns to Peter and tells him to strengthen his brothers when he turned back. The turning back is a reference to Peter's triple denial and the need to turn back from that. Peter is being given special authority over the other Apostles. In Matthew, this passing of authority is found in the Keys of the Kingdom passage in chapter 16. That particular passage speaks of the power of the underworld opposing the Church (like the Satan sifting the Apostles like wheat saying). In John, we find this same mandate in chapter 21 (which has a triple question of whether Peter loves Him, reminding us of the "turning back" saying). These three Gospels all affirm a special role for Peter in the Church.

Immediately after this, Jesus speaks of being ready for what was coming. Earlier, He had told them to trust in God, carrying no purses or other provisions. Now He tells them to bring a sword. They respond that they have two, and Jesus answers, "It is enough."

This is a very confusing passage. Why would Jesus command them to arm themselves? He rejected violence when He was arrested. Maybe He was simply saying, "Be ready for what is coming." The Apostles then interpret His sayings in an overly literal manner (as when He said to be careful of the yeast of the Pharisees and they thought He was talking about bread). In this case, the phrase, "It is enough," might very well be an expression of frustration at their misunderstanding what He was really saying. It would be comparable to saying, "All right, already; I've had enough of this nonsense."

In the Garden of Gethsamene

JESUS leads Peter, James and John into the Garden of Gethsamene. The name "Gethsamene" means "oil press," and there is archaeological evidence that there were oil presses in the area around the garden. He leaves His Disciples at the entrance and goes in further to pray to the Father. This is the only Gospel that speaks of His being strengthened by an angel. It is also the only Gospel that speaks of His sweating blood. This phrase could mean one of two things. It could mean that He was sweating so much that it almost seemed as if He were bleeding, or it could mean that blood was pouring out from His skin. This occasionally happens when someone is highly traumatized. These two ideas, the angels and the sweat, are not found in all of the ancient manuscripts of this Gospel. Some people feel that they might have been added by a scribe later on.

When Jesus is arrested in the garden, He asks Judas if he was going to betray Him with a kiss. This was the way that Judas intended to point Jesus out to the soldiers in a rather dark garden. Yet, in Luke, Judas doesn't actually kiss Him. This gesture might have been a bit too touchy, feely for the stoic Luke.

Luke the physician, as we have already seen, then has Jesus heal the slave whose ear had been cut off.

The Trials and the Passion

A S we have already seen, Pilate sends Jesus to Herod after which Pilate and Herod become the best of friends. It is Herod's soldiers, however, and not Pilate's soldiers who mock and torment Jesus. Herod's soldiers were not Romans. Pilate also openly declares Jesus' innocence (23:13ff). These details might be phrased this way to remind Roman officials that Christians, like Christ, were really innocent and should not be persecuted.

The greatest difference in the Passion narrative is that Jesus confronts the weeping women of Jerusalem (23:27ff). Women are once again playing a significant role in the narrative. Jesus expresses His compassion for them.

In Luke, Jesus also prays for the forgiveness of those who were crucifying Him. At the very minute that they are hatefully hurting Him, He is worried about them. It is as if someone were to slap a person across the face, and the injured party asked, "Did you hurt your hand?"

It is only in Luke that we have one of the two thieves defend Jesus. (Traditionally he is called Dismas.) He is told that he would be in paradise that very day. (Remember how the scene forms the closing frame of Jesus' outreach to the poor and broken. The opening frame was the invitation of the shepherds to adore the baby Jesus. From beginning to end in this Gospel, Jesus reaches out to those who most need Him.) Furthermore, this is another example of how the promises of salvation would be fulfilled immediately (as it was with Zaccheus).

While Jesus is on the Cross, we do not hear Him cry out, "My God, my God, why have You forsaken Me?" This was the first line of Psalm 22, and Jesus was expressing both His feelings of abandonment and His trust that God would deliver Him, a sentiment found at the end of this psalm. The difficulty is that Luke's Gentile readers might not have understood the nuances of this quotation. It might have seemed scandalously weak to them, so Luke dropped it. Rather than doubting the Father's intention, Jesus places His spirit in the Father's hands (23:46). The Greek philosophers reading Luke's Gospel would have been impressed with Jesus' equanimity in the face of torment. (There are other passages where Luke softens the emotion of Jesus' reaction.)

The centurion's words under the Cross are quite interesting. In Matthew and Mark, he proclaims that Jesus is the "Son of God." In Jewish circles, the phrase "Son of God" meant "a hero." Since the man was a centurion, however, and therefore a pagan, the phrase "Son of God" took on a new meaning for it would mean more than the old Jewish meaning, it meant that He truly was the Son of God as we understand it.

Luke might have been worried that his Gentile Christian readers would not understand this statement and might interpret it as saying that Jesus was one of the minor deities of which they had too many. Luke, therefore, took another direction with the centurion's proclamation. He had him say, "Certainly this man was innocent" (23:47). Once again, we have a Roman official recognizing how Jesus was innocent, and by implication how His followers, Christians, were innocent.

Questions

1. If Jerusalem is such a holy city, then why did so few of its people follow Jesus?

2. We know that Luke loved food. What did it represent for him? What does that say about the way he speaks about the Last Supper?

3. What does Christian leadership mean?

4. Does God sometimes send an angel (a moment of consolation, a friend, a sign) to strengthen us when we need it most?

5. When we are going through difficult times, do we think only of ourselves or do we still reach out to others to offer them consolation and assistance?

Prayer

Lord, teach me to be generous, even when I am tempted to pull back out of fear and mistrust. May my own sufferings teach me to be compassionate with others who are also suffering. May I even offer up some of my difficulties as a sacrifice of love for them.

Conclusion:

Luke's Original Message

THESE many passages help us to see how Luke took the story of Jesus that had been passed down to him and shaped it in such a way that could best serve his audience. Sometimes, it was a question of changing a phrase or adding another detail to an already existent story. Other times, it was adding a whole new story from his original source (which is not to say that the story was not true, only that it was most useful in developing Luke's themes).

We saw how Jesus is presented almost as a new philosopher who teaches about mercy and compassion. We discovered that while the Gospel was intended for a fairly educated audience, it was the *anawim*, the poor ones of God, who are held up as exemplars of true discipleship. It is easier for them to embrace Jesus than for those who are better off. They recognize their weakness and dependence. Those better off often feel themselves to be self-sufficient. This was not why the rich were blessed with material goods. The well off were given riches by God so that they would use them to assist those people who were less well off. Tertullian, a writer in the early Church, states that what was in excess is robbed from the poor.

Luke demonstrates some Stoic tendencies. We see that God has a plan for all of us and we will find joy if we discern and obey that plan. This Gospel recognizes the need to bow to God's will for God is both king of our lives and a loving parent who only wants what is good for us. We could even say that Jesus heals the wound that Adam, the first man, caused by his disobedience through His own obedience and trust of the will of the Father.

The Blessed Virgin Mary is also portrayed as the model of obedience and submission to the will of God. Unlike Mark in which the family of Jesus has a difficult time accepting who Jesus is, in this Gospel Mary is the perfect disciple. Even though her thoughts (heart) were cut to the quick by the sword of discernment, she believed, for she was among the Disciples at Pentecost.

Women in general are treated with much more respect than in Matthew or Mark. We saw the pattern of having a story or parable about a man quickly followed up by a story about a woman. Women followed Jesus and ministered to Him and His Disciples. A number of them also showed up after the Resurrection and gave witness to it.

Foreigners are treated with more respect. They are often seen as examples of faith. While Luke respected the Jews and Jewish tradition, he doesn't take his eyes off the fact that his readers were not Jews and therefore had to feel welcomed in the community.

We witnessed Luke's incredible talent as an artist. He shapes the three accounts of the Resurrection to provide an outline of the Christian life: first we hear about Jesus from others, then we encounter Him in sacrament and word, and finally we recognize His presence everywhere. We also saw his talent in the construction of the infancy narratives as a diptych. The stories of the birth of John the Baptist and Jesus are presented as parallels, but that of John is great while that of Jesus is greater. It was in the infancy narratives, though, that we had to wonder a bit whether Luke considered his primary obligation to be a historian or to be an artist. We saw how he probably borrowed the canticles of Mary, Zechariah and Simeon from pre-existent sources and put these words in their mouths because he felt that this is the tenor of what these characters would have said. But we also had to wonder about the historicity of a couple of details of the story (the fact that the holy family is portrayed as living originally in Nazareth and not Bethlehem as it is in Matthew and the presentation of the story of the universal census which does not seem to be credible).

Luke's version of the story of Jesus is beautiful. It also reminds us that its message must be available to whichever audience it is being presented. We shouldn't make the Gospel say whatever we want it to say, but the message of Jesus is certainly rich enough that it can speak to any culture in any era and offer salvation to all.

Finally, Luke certainly reminds us of our obligation to preach the forgiveness of sins. We are called to be Jesus' messengers.

Whether we do that in simple, quiet ways or we sell everything and go to distant lands to preach, we are called. So many people do not know about God's mercy and love and compassion. So many are trapped in lifestyles that leave them lonely and experiencing a sense of meaninglessness. They need us not only to proclaim the Gospel in our own lives, but also to renew the Acts of the Apostles, spreading the Gospel once again from its spiritual base all the way to the political and commercial center of our modern world.

Prayer

St. Luke, pray for us.

Part IV

The Gospel of John

Chapter 1

The Text

THERE were four Gospels written between 70 and 90 A.D. Three of these Gospels are quite similar: Matthew, Mark and Luke. They are called the Synoptic Gospels. The word synoptic is a combination of two Greek words: sun = with and optic = eye. It literally means to see things with one eye, or from one point of view. They are so similar because Matthew and Luke borrowed extensively from the Gospel of Mark.

The Gospel of John is quite different. It was probably written around 90 A.D., the last of the Gospels to be written. It presents a Jesus Who is much more divine than the one found in the other Gospels. This Jesus is the One Who reveals the truths of God. This is why He teaches so much, for His mission is not to "do;" it is to "reveal." It is not uncommon in this Gospel to hear twenty or thirty or even forty verses of teaching in a row. Jesus knows everything and is in control of everything until the very moment of His death. There are no "miracles," for in this Gospel they are called "signs" (actions that point to a greater reality) and not "miracles" (deeds of wonder).

Even though this Gospel was written after the others, John does not seem to have borrowed from those Gospels. Did its author not know about the existence of the other Gospels, or did he ignore them?

Over this past century, many scholars have addressed these questions. They have concluded that this Gospel was written for a group of Christians who were called the community of the Beloved Disciple. The Beloved Disciple is the hero of this Gospel for he follows Jesus as an act of love. He is compared positively to the Apostles who never seem to get their act together. This community seems to have valued mystical love more than the others. They were charismatic, not demonstrating much respect for apostolic authority. The word "apostle" in fact never appears in this Gospel nor does the list of the twelve Apostles.

From various hints in the Gospel, we can determine that this was probably a Jewish Christian community. The Gospel shows familiarity with Jewish customs. What is odd, though, is that the

Gospel implies that the time for these traditions has passed; Jesus has replaced things with His own person. Which group of Jews were more willing to abandon the traditions of the elders? It was the Greek-speaking Jews who were called the Hellenists.

Thus, the community of the Beloved was probably a group of Greek-speaking Jews who were not part of the mainline Church. They were more egalitarian than other Christians (who by this time were establishing a hierarchy in the Church). They believed that Jesus was the answer to all their questions. There is, in fact, only one sin in this entire Gospel, not to believe that Jesus is the Son of God.

Problems with the Text

ALL of the New Testament writings have questions about whether one or another of its passages is authentic, but it usually is a question of a verse or two. The Gospel of John is a bit different because there are a number of significant issues to address. This type of an investigation is called textual criticism.

Starting from the end of the Gospel, it seems as if there are two endings. Chapter 20 closes with a passage that would appear to be the last verses of the Gospel (20:30-31), but then there is another entire chapter with a second ending (21:24-25). Why?

First of all, the vocabulary and grammar and theology of chapter 21 are all consistent with the rest of the Gospel, so it was obviously produced by the same author as the rest of the Gospel. Chapter 21 appears in all of the ancient manuscripts, so if it was added to the Gospel, it was added very early. How can we explain the double ending? The best explanation is that it was, in fact, written by the same author as the rest of the Gospel but that it was added to the Gospel to address certain problems that had not been dealt with sufficiently in the Gospel. Chapter 21, in fact, deals with two issues: the need for authority in the community and the death of the Beloved Disciple. (This material will be examined at greater length later in this book.)

A second textual question is found in the Last Supper discourse. This is an extensive series of passages that Jesus proclaims as a type of last testament. The problem is that at the end of chapter 14 (verse 31), Jesus seems to be ending His discourse.

Then He continues to speak for the next three chapters. Either He was like those preachers who say that they have one more point to make and then go on and on, or the material after 14:31 was added on. Once again, though, if it was added, it was not by another author. As the community gathered materials over the years between the Ascension (c. 30 A.D.) and when the Gospel was written (c. 90 A.D.), it produced various collections of materials. An earlier version of the Last Supper discourse ended at the end of chapter 14, and a later version continued through chapter 17. The author of the Gospel used the later version when he wrote the Gospel.

The textual problem in 8:1-11 is a bit different. This is the story of a woman caught in adultery. This story is not found in a number of important manuscripts. If one takes it out, the material that remains follows in logical order. This means that this story was probably added after the Gospel was first issued.

Then there is the theology. In the Gospel of John, there is only one sin: not to believe that Jesus is the Son of God. Yet, this is a story that deals with the sin of adultery.

Furthermore, in 8:2, we hear that Jesus was teaching, but the text doesn't give us a single verse of what He said (while all throughout the Gospel, every time He speaks He goes on for verses and verses).

All of this makes us believe that this story was added to the Gospel. Its message actually seems to fit in better to the Gospel of Luke than John. It deals with the plight of a woman and of God's willingness to forgive sinners, both of which are themes found throughout Luke. Why is it here? It is possible that a scribe came across this story and realized that it was not to be found in any of the other Gospels. Rather than lose this story, the scribe placed it in the Gospel he happened to be copying at the time: that of John. (Remember, if the scribe was copying this on a scroll, he could not have backed up and put it in Luke where it would have fit better.)

There is another textual problem at the beginning of chapter 6. We hear that Jesus crossed to the other side of the Sea of Galilee. The only problem was that in chapter 5 Jesus was in Jerusalem which is nowhere near the Sea of Galilee. This doesn't make sense. It wouldn't be a problem, however, if chapters 5 and 6 were inverted. Someone must have changed the order of the chapters. We will see why later when we study the multiplication of loaves and fish.

The final textual question is found in chapter 1: the Prologue. This is a beautiful hymn about the eternal Word of God which becomes flesh. It is made up of a series of sections, alternating between poetry and prose. The poetry sections speak about the Word of God while the prose sections speak about the role of John the Baptist. While the Gospel of John is closely identified with the theology of the Word of God, it is really only found in the Prologue. At the same time, the material about John the Baptist is consistent with the rest of the Gospel. From this observation, we can make a proposal. It is possible that the author of this Gospel borrowed a pre-existent poem about the Word of God which he used as an introduction to the Gospel. He wanted to tie this poem tightly to the Gospel, however, so he put in the prose sections about John the Baptist, material that was consistent with the rest of the Gospel.

Just by looking at these questions, we should get the impression that this Gospel had a long and somewhat complicated history. Even if it was written around 90 A.D., the community which produced it had been working on its ideas for decades. This long period of development helps to explain its profound theology and symbolism. These are so remarkably developed that St. Augustine once said of it that the Gospel is shallow enough for a child to play in but profound enough for an elephant to swim in. There are layers and layers of meaning in this Gospel which is artistically portrayed with the symbol of an angel (because its symbolism soars to the heavens).

Question

1. Did John write all of the material found in this Gospel?

Prayer

God, when I look back in my life, it's sometimes difficult to sort out how things really happened. Give me insight into what is important to remember and what I should let go of.

Chapter 2

The Community of the Beloved Disciple

The Man Born Blind

WHY was the Gospel of John written? To answer this, we should look at the Gospel itself to see if there is any evidence there to help us to sort it out.

A good starting point is the story of the man born blind (chapter 9). There are a number of questions that arise as we look at the text. First of all, the Gospel of John centers on Jesus. Yet, Jesus all but disappears throughout the central two-thirds of this story. Why? Then when the man is brought before the Jewish officials for questioning, he is brought to the Pharisees. Where is the other major group of Jewish officials, the Sadducees? Third, we do not hear until verse 14 that this miracle occurred on the Sabbath. Why did it take so long for the author to state this? Fourth, when the Pharisees call in the parents of the man born blind for questioning, they do not say anything because it had already been agreed that anyone who said that Jesus was the Christ would be expelled from the synagogue. There are actually two problems here. First of all, this is occurring in Jerusalem. The place that one would be afraid of being expelled from was the temple, not the synagogue. Second, the decision to expel Christians from the synagogue was made much later, around 80 A.D. What is going on?

We can respond to all of these difficulties by stating that this is a story being told at two levels. At the surface level, this is a physical miracle that Jesus performed in 30 A.D. Jesus healed a man born blind on the Sabbath, and this got Him and the man into trouble with the Pharisees. At the second level, this is the story of a community that was spiritually blind and which came to know the light of the world. They were punished for their belief in Jesus as the Christ and were therefore expelled from the synagogue (sometime around 80 A.D.).

Why were they expelled? This part of the story dates to the decade after the destruction of the temple in Jerusalem by the Romans in 70 A.D. Before it was destroyed, one could believe almost anything and still call oneself a Jew as long as one wor-shiped Yahweh, the God of Israel. There were the Sadducees, the Pharisees, the Zealots, the Essenes, and even the Nazarenes (people who believed that Jesus of Nazareth was the Messiah). After the destruction of the temple, the rabbis who were Pharisees decided that they had to define what it meant to be a Jew. They made three major decisions. They rejected the Greek translation of the Old Testament that was in use at this time. This translation was called the Septuagint. It was rejected because Christians were using some of its passages to show that Jesus was the Messiah. The second decision was that they decreed that only those books written in Hebrew or Aramaic would be con-sidered to be part of the Bible (thus excluding 1 and 2 Mac-cabees, Tobit, Judith, Wisdom, Sirach and Baruch, books that Catholics call the Deutero-canonical books and which Protestants call the Apocrypha).

Finally, the rabbis added a prayer to their 18 benedictions, a type of prayer of the faithful. This prayer called for the death of heretics and the eternal damnation of Christians. (Although we are not sure of exactly how this prayer was phrased in its early years, this was its basic sense).

If one was suspected of being a Christian, one was asked to say that prayer. If one hesitated or refused, one was expelled from the synagogue. This meant that one lost one's community of worship, and one also lost one's own family who would say the prayer of the dead over the expelled person. (Remember the scene from *Fiddler on the Roof* when one of the daughters mar-ries a Christian.) One even faced death because there were only two legitimate religions in the Roman empire: Judaism and the emperor cult. If one was no longer a Jew, then one would have to worship the emperor. If one refused to do that, then one would be put to death. This third decision endangered the very lives of early Christians.

We should now look at the account quickly to examine some of its symbolism. The account begins with Jesus encoun-tering a man who had been born blind. Jesus' Disciples ask whether the man was blind as a punishment for his sins or for the sins of his parents. This is terribly rude for the man was not deaf, he was blind. He heard what the Disciples were say-ing about him.

Jesus refuses to play this game. He answers that this was so that God's work could be seen through Him. One can almost see the smile on the man's face. Jesus had already begun to heal him spiritually even before He heals him physically.

Jesus then speaks about being the light of the world. This is called high Christology. Christology is what one says about Jesus. Low Christology is when one speaks about Jesus' human-ity; high Christology is when one speaks about Jesus' divinity.

Jesus then performs an action which could be described as being very low Christology. He spits on the dirt and makes mud and rubs it on the man's eyes. This is something that one would do if one were a healer in the first century A.D., but Jesus did this on the Sabbath, and Pharisees would consider this action to be a sin for they considered it to be work. There were, in fact, actu-ally two sins: making mud and healing the man.

Jesus orders the man to go to the pool of Siloam. He goes, washes, and is healed. Notice how quickly and easily He heals the man.

When the man returns, no one recognizes him. His neighbors never really knew him; they only knew his disability. (This is quite common even in today's world.) When they ask who healed him, he answers, "the man named Jesus." This is a low Christological statement.

In verse 13, the man is brought before the Pharisees. Theoretically, he would have been brought before the Sanhedrin which consisted both of Pharisees and Sadducees. Here the Sadducees are not even mentioned, for this part of the story takes place at its second level, around 80 A.D., when the Sadducees no longer existed.

In verse 14, we hear that it was the Sabbath. In the Synoptics, if Jesus were doing something on the Sabbath, we would hear about it in the first verse of the account. In this account, we hear about it in the middle of the story. There is a subtle message here. For Jesus, it didn't make a difference what day it was for He was intent on healing the man. For the Pharisees, it was important, for they objected to the work that Jesus was doing. The man had been blind since his birth. They couldn't understand why Jesus wouldn't wait another day. But Jesus wouldn't make the man wait another second, for he had been waiting since birth to see.

The Pharisees were confused. They were quite sure that Jesus was a sinner for He had done work on the Sabbath, and sinners cannot heal people. They therefore asked the man what he thought about Jesus, and he answers, "He is a prophet." Notice that the Christology is a bit higher than in the first statement the man had made about Jesus.

In the central scene of the chapter, the parents of the man born blind are brought before the Pharisees. They are questioned as to what happened to their son. They respond that he is old enough and they should ask him. As parents, their natural response should have been to try to protect their son. Instead, they push him in front of a speeding truck because of their fear of being thrown out of the synagogue. (Remember, this is at the second, later level of the story.)

The Pharisees therefore call the man back in and tell him to give glory to God for they knew that Jesus was a sinner. In this Gospel, certain words will recur over and over again to make a specific point. In this chapter, the word "sin" is repeated. The man born blind is accused of being a sinner. Jesus is accused of the same thing. Yet, by the end of the story, it turns out that it is the Pharisees who are sinners.

The man born blind begins to challenge the Pharisees, asking them whether they wanted to become His disciples as well. This man was uneducated; the Pharisees were highly educated. Yet, he was able to see the truth better than they were. He eventually calls Jesus "a man from God," another heightening of the Christology.

The Pharisees expel the man from their midst, and when this happens, Jesus goes over to speak to him. Jesus asks him whether he believes in the Son of Man and He identifies Himself as that person. The man responds, "I do believe, Lord," and he worships Him. "Lord" is a title used for Yahweh in the Old Testament, so the man is professing his belief in Jesus' divinity. This is reinforced when he falls down on his knees and worships Him, something that one only does to God.

It makes sense that the man would recognize Jesus' divinity when he was expelled from the synagogue. While he was still in the synagogue, the man/the community could not affirm Jesus' divinity. That would have gotten him killed. When he was expelled, there was nothing more that they could do to him, so he could openly state what he already believed in his heart. This is the highest of Christologies, for the man was saying that Jesus was one with the Father.

The story closes with Jesus confronting the Pharisees and accusing them of rejection of what they knew was true, and this makes them sinners.

These five scenes (Jesus and the man, the man and the Pharisees, the Pharisees and the man's parents, the man and the Pharisees, and Jesus and the man) are written in a form of literature called a chiasm. This is a literary structure with an odd number of sections in which the first and the last are related, the second and the second last, etc. The climax of the story is in the central section. In this case, as one can see above, it is the section in which the Pharisees interrogate the parents. Why was that section so important? Who do the parents represent?

When the rabbis decided to exclude Christians from the synagogue, there must have been some Christians who hid their identity (like the parents). It is possible that they even had good reasons. They might have done it to protect their families, or possibly because they thought that the persecution wouldn't last all that long, or they might have just been afraid. Yet, to the Johannine community, they were traitors. This is why the central section of this chiasm involves these parents who represent hidden Christians, those who denied who they were. John was trying to tell them to confess their faith publicly.

To conclude, this story has two levels. Jesus really performed a miracle in 30 A.D. But the community also paid the price for giving witness to their faith in 80 A.D. Both levels of this story are true.

One more observation could be made about this story. Remember that we observed that Jesus did not appear in the central portion of the story. At its second level of meaning, it refers to what Christians experienced when they were suffering (like the man who was expelled from the synagogue). It seemed as if Jesus was so far away. Yet, when we suffer, Jesus is suffering with us. This is what we saw in the Acts of the Apostles when Jesus revealed Himself to Paul on the road to Damascus. Jesus asked Paul why he was persecuting Him. Paul was persecuting Christians, but Jesus called it persecuting Him for when we suffer, He is one with us. This also explains why the interrogation of the man born blind and his parents vaguely resembles the trial of Jesus. Jesus joined His sufferings to ours as we join our sufferings to His.

Questions

1. What does it mean to be "blind" in this account? To be a "sinner"?
2. Trace the development of the blind man's faith in terms of low and high Christology.
3. Describe the use of a chiasm in this story.

Prayer

Open my eyes, O Lord, to Your message and Your call. May I have the courage to give witness to my faith always and everywhere.

Chapter 3

Matrimonial Symbolism

The Roles of John the Baptist

WE have already seen references to John the Baptist in the Prologue. He is also spoken of in the rest of chapter 1 and in chapter 3. What is odd, though, is the role he plays. All the Gospels agree that he prepares the way for the Lord. The Synoptic Gospels have him do that by calling people to repentance. In the Gospel of John, he does that by giving witness to the fact that Jesus is the Messiah.

When the Jewish leaders sent emissaries to John to ask him who he was, he did not deny but he confessed, "I am not the Messiah." Notice the emphasis on his giving witness by confessing the truth, but also notice the strange formulation of his response. The emissaries did not ask who he wasn't, they asked who he was. Why would he answer their question in the negative?

As they continue to press him for information, he informs them that he came to prepare the way for the One Who followed him Whose sandals he was not worthy to unstrap. This statement has two levels of meaning. It means that he felt himself unworthy to touch the least significant of His garments, but it also refers to matrimonial symbolism.

When a man died in Israel without having had children, his widow was to marry the next of kin. If that man refused, she would call him to stand before the elders of the town and have him repeat his refusal. When he did that, she would spit in his face and then either her sandal or his was untied as a sign of giving up the right to marry the widow.

Israel had been married to God in the Old Covenant. God had not died, but she had treated God as if He were dead, so she might as well have been a widow. John could not marry Israel for he was not the Messiah; Jesus was the "next of kin" to God. He was the One Who would establish a new marriage, a new covenant between God and Israel.

This symbolism continues in chapter 3 when John speaks of the joy he had at hearing the bridegroom's voice. This is an allusion to the words of the prophet Jeremiah. Three times the prophet predicted that the destruction that would come upon Israel would be so severe that one would no longer hear the voice of the bride nor the voice of the bridegroom. He was saying that it would be so bad that there would no longer be marriages; therefore no children, no future. Then, when Jeremiah predicts the new covenant between God and Israel, he says that God will relent and one will once again hear the voice of the bride and the bridegroom. By having John the Baptist say this, he is saying that the promise of the new covenant would be fulfilled in the person of Jesus.

John also identifies himself as the friend of the bridegroom. We would call that person the best man. In the Jewish world, one of the best man's jobs was to physically carry the bride on a platform to the groom, just as John the Baptist had led Israel to Jesus.

John also says that Jesus must increase while he must decrease. The word in Greek for increase is the same word as "multiply," just like God's command to "go forth and multiply." This is almost a wedding toast in which the best man wishes that the bride and groom have many children.

The Wedding Feast of Cana

ANOTHER scene that has matrimonial symbolism is that of the wedding feast of Cana. The story begins, "On the third day." As soon as we hear those words, we think of the resurrection, which gives us a good indication that this story is speaking about more than wine.

We hear that the mother of Jesus is there with Jesus and His Disciples. Mary is identified as "the mother of Jesus." Her name is never used in the account. In this Gospel, when a person is identified by a title and not a name (e.g., the man born blind, the Beloved Disciple), that person is playing a symbolic role.

Mary tells her son that they have no more wine, and His response is, "What is it to Me and You, woman, My hour has not yet come." This is not as harsh as it sounds in English. Jesus is simply telling His mother that it was none of their business. What is odd is the words found at the end. He speaks of His "hour." In this Gospel, this refers to His "hour of glory." Usually, when we hear the word "glory," we think of power or magnificence. If that were the case here, then the hour of glory would be the Resurrection. In this Gospel, the word "glory" is redefined as the outpouring of love. The hour of glory is thus the Cross. That is the moment when we most clearly see the love of God.

Mary asked for a little wine. Why would Jesus answer that it would bring about His hour, His Cross? Isn't that a little over the top? But not really. If Jesus does something about this wine, then it will lead Him to the Cross.

Still, Mary tells the servants, "Do whatever He tells you." She is a parent who loves her son so much that she calls Him to the Cross for she wants Him to be the most loving person possible.

We hear that there were six stone jars there used for ceremonial washings. Seven is the perfect number in the Bible, so this custom must have been lacking in some way (for there were only six jars). Each jar held around 25 gallons, which makes 150 gallons of water made into wine. That is a lot of wine, too much. This is especially true when one considers the Jewish attitude toward drunkenness; it was abhorred.

The servants take the water made into wine to the steward who then calls the groom. He asks why he saved the good wine for last when usually one serves the good wine first and then when people won't notice it as much, the not so good wine. The first wine represents the Old Covenant, while the second, better wine represents the New Covenant. John is saying that God left the best for last. The abundance of wine in the Old Testament was associated with the heavenly banquet. Jesus was preparing not only this couple's wedding feast, but also the heavenly wedding feast. We get to that feast through the cross (which is why He mentioned "His hour" to His mother).

And what is Mary's role in this passage. She is described as "the mother." In the Old Testament, the mother of the king was the queen mother and her most important responsibility was to prepare the wedding feast for her son, which is exactly what Mary did in this passage.

This is described as being Jesus' first sign of glory. It is not called a miracle because people often become too focused on extraordinary and miraculous deeds. It is called a sign to remind us that it calls us to a greater level of mystery.

The Samaritan Woman at the Well

THE next story with significant matrimonial symbolism is that of the Samaritan woman at the well. In order to understand that story at all its levels, we have to know that the well story is a common leitmotif in the Old Testament. Leitmotifs are recurring patterns in music or literature. The well story has the basic pattern of a man going to a well where a women gives him water. He takes the water, marries the woman, and they live happily ever after.

There are several examples of this motif in the Old Testament. The first involves Isaac. He doesn't go to the well himself. Eliezer, Abraham's servant, goes for him. When he arrives at the well, Rebekah gives him water and then waters his camels. Each camel can drink 35 gallons, so this is a truly generous woman, generous enough to become a matriarch of Israel. Why did Isaac not go to the well himself? Probably because he is such a weak character, always being used or abused by someone (e.g., his wife and younger son Jacob who steal his final blessing from the elder son Esau).

The second episode involves Jacob. When he goes to the well, there is a large stone over the mouth of the well, so large that it usually takes several men to move it. Jacob is able to move it himself. The well represents either the woman or the womb, or in this case both.

He has to work for his uncle for seven years in order to marry his beloved Rachel, but this uncle cheats him by substituting Rachel's older sister Leah on the wedding night. Therefore he has to work for another seven years to marry Rachel. This difficulty reminds us of the well that was all but closed.

But the well also stands for fertility. Leah, her sister, Leah's servant and Rachel's servant all have a number of children while Rachel is barren. Finally, she gives birth to Joseph, but dies giving birth to Benjamin, her second born. Like the well, her womb was all but closed.

The third use of this leitmotif is the story of Moses and his wife. He goes to the well and falls asleep. The seven daughters of Jethro come to the well to water their flocks, but they are chased away by evil shepherds. He wakes up and defends them, just as he was always defending the powerless.

The fourth use is the story of Ruth and Boaz. Ruth does not offer Boaz water; he offers her water, for she was a foreigner and it was not her water to give.

What, then, is Jesus doing at the well? This is all part of the matrimonial symbolism of this Gospel. Israel had been married to God in the old covenant, but the Samaritans were not part of that marriage. Through the Samaritan woman, they are being invited into a new covenant/marriage with God. That is why Jesus speaks of the woman's husbands, saying that she had had five and the man she was now with was not even her husband. That makes six, and Jesus would be the seventh, for it was through him that God would marry the Samaritans. (This is why the woman's name is never mentioned, for she represents all of her people.)

Having said all of this, let's go back to the beginning of the story and determine the meaning of its symbolism. We hear that Jesus went to the well at noon and the Samaritan woman was there to get water. This is very odd, for in hot climates one goes to the well early in the morning before it gets too hot to carry the water. She was there early so that she could avoid other people who might gossip about her past.

Jesus asks her for a drink and she asks why a Jew would ask for water from a Samaritan. Jews and Samaritans hated each other and had very little to do with each other. But even beyond that, the woman knew what Jewish men did at wells: that is where they met their wives. The one thing that this woman had more than enough of was husbands, so she was standoffish.

Jesus goes on to offer her living water. Living water could be water that is flowing or water that gives life. The woman understands the former and she asks Jesus Who He thinks He is. Does He think that He is better than Jacob their ancestor? There is a good deal of irony in this Gospel, for of course He is greater than Jacob.

At this point, Jesus offers the woman life-giving water that would spring up inside of her. Jesus is offering her a life so profound that it would flow out from her heart. The woman responds, "Sir, give me this water so I don't have to keep coming to this well." Jesus is offering eternal life, and all she wants is indoor plumbing. (But aren't we like that, often only thinking about what God can do for us when we need something.) Yet, even without realizing it, the woman was saying more than she realized. She calls Jesus "sir," which in Greek is *"Kyrios,"* a word that could also be translated as "Lord." She was already professing her faith, even though she did not know it yet.

This is when Jesus asks her to call her husband. She says that she does not have "a husband." He responds that she is right. She's had five, and the man she is with now isn't her husband.

She asks Jesus, "Are You a prophet? We worship on this mountain (Mount Gerazim, the mountain where Samaritans still worship) and you worship on Mount Zion. Which is it?"

Jesus answers that from now on people will worship God in Spirit and Truth. The Spirit, for Christians, is the Holy Spirit. The truth is Jesus. We worship God in and through Jesus and the Holy Spirit. We even hear this in the doxology at the end of the Eucharistic Prayer which states, "In Him, and through Him, and with Him, in the unity of the Holy Spirit . . ."

The woman then asks Jesus if He is the coming Messiah. The Samaritan Messiah was called the *Ta'eb* and he was very different from the Jewish Messiah. The Jewish Messiah was a conqueror. The Samaritan Messiah was one who revealed the secrets of God. What is that secret? It is how much God loves us. God loves us so much that He has His own Son die out of love for us.

Jesus' response to the woman is not even subtle. He says, "The one speaking with you, I am." The words "I am" was the name of God in the Old Testament. Jesus is saying that He is one with the Father.

At this point, the woman leaves her jar there (for she doesn't need it any more because she is filled to overflowing with His love) and she goes back into her village. There she tells her listeners, "Come and meet someone who told me everything that I ever did." This is the same woman who only a short time before had avoided these people because of what she had done. Now that she had experienced God's love, she could take a risk.

In the meantime, the Disciples returned and asked Jesus if He wanted any of the food that they brought. Jesus told them that He had food of which they did not know. He is always speaking at a higher spiritual level while the Disciples (and others like the Samaritan woman) understood things at a material level.

Jesus also quotes a saying, "Four months more and the harvest." He tells them to look up and see that the fields were already white for the harvest. Some translations say, "the fields are glistening," or that they are "ripe." This is a bit of a mistranslation for the Greek word is *"leukos"* which means white. Jesus was not pointing at the wheat fields; He was pointing at the Samaritans coming out of the village who wore white garments. They were the harvest.

The Samaritans came out and listened to Jesus and said that at first they believed because of what the woman had said, but now they believed for themselves that He was the Savior of the world. Interestingly, the title "Savior" of the world was a favorite title for the Roman emperors. John was telling his readers that Jesus was the only true Savior.

What great miracle did Jesus perform to bring this woman around? He treated her with more respect than she thought that she deserved. By treating her this way, He made her want to be what Jesus thought of her.

The Anointing

THE next matrimonial symbolism is found in the anointing of Jesus (chapter 12). Mary, the sister of Martha and Lazarus, anoints the feet of Jesus with a liter of pure aromatic nard. This is an incredibly expensive ointment. The plant used to make it only grows in the Himalayan mountains. Judas even says it could have been sold for 300 denarii. A denarius was a day's wage, so this is almost a year's salary for this one bottle of ointment. This is an incredibly extravagant gesture.

Jesus interprets this as an act of love to prepare Him for His burial. But Judas objects stating that it could have been sold and used to feed the poor. The text tells us that he only wanted to steal the money, but one can also discern another reason. He wanted to do charity; Mary wanted to love the person in front of her. Sometimes we do good deeds for our own benefit, so that people will think well of us. St. Vincent de Paul once said that we can only pray that the poor will forgive us our "charity." True charity is loving the people we meet, and making them feel that they are loved.

The Crucifixion

THE crucifixion in John continues this symbolism. We hear that the soldiers wanted to break the legs of those who had been crucified. On the cross, one tended not to die from loss of blood. One died from suffocation. Because one's body was distended, one could no longer catch one's breath unless one pushed up on one's legs. When one was too tired to push up anymore, then that person died. There were cases in which a person survived for over a week on the cross. This Good Friday, however, was the beginning of Passover, and so the soldiers were breaking the legs so that the prisoners would die immediately and their bodies could be taken off the cross before sunset.

When the soldier reached Jesus, he found that He was already dead, so he took his lance and His side and immediately blood and water flowed out. This casts an allusion to the creation of the first woman Eve. God put Adam in a deep sleep (not unlike the fact that Jesus was dead) and opened his side (like the soldier did to Jesus). The blood stands for the Eucharist and the water stands for Baptism, the two sacraments that we know that this community celebrated. Jesus married the Church on the Cross.

But in Jewish marriages, if a man dies without having children, his widow has to marry the next of kin. This is part of the reason why Jesus adopts the Beloved Disciple as His brother. He was to care for His mother, but he was also to marry the widow (the Church) so that he might bear children who would bear the deceased's name (Christians).

Furthermore, the Beloved is never named in this Gospel. He is only known by his title which means that he is playing a symbolic role. Who is the beloved? Ultimately, we are! We are to bear children (spiritually) who bear Christ's name.

Jesus is buried by Joseph of Arimithea and Nicodemus in a garden, anointed with a mixture of myrrh and aloes.

The garden is intended to be the Garden of Eden, for the death and resurrection of Jesus produced a new birth, a new creation.

The myrrh and aloes are an allusion to Psalm 45 where the bridegroom's robes are fragrant with myrrh and aloes.

The Resurrection Narratives

CHAPTERS 20 and 21 of John continue some of this symbolism when they present the Resurrection stories as well as presenting other symbolic teachings.

We hear that Mary Magdalene went out to the tomb early on Easter morning (when one can see the light on the horizon but cannot yet see the sun). Mary goes alone for she represents the Church looking for her beloved. Two angels announce Jesus' Resurrection, so she runs and tells Peter and the Beloved.

These two Disciples run to the tomb, and the Beloved arrives first (not because he is younger, but because he is in love). He awaits Peter outside of the tomb because love bows to authority. Peter enters and sees, while the Beloved enters, sees, and believes. The Beloved believes for he is seeing this all with his heart.

Mary then searches the garden for her beloved. She sees Jesus but does not recognize Him for she thinks that He is the gardener. She asks Him where He has taken Jesus. This scene reminds us of the Song of Songs where the lover looks for the beloved and asks the city guards where they have taken him. Jesus calls her by name and she recognizes Him (for the sheep know the Good Shepherd's voice). She tries to cling to Jesus, but He forbids it. She (the Church) cannot hold onto Jesus bodily. She will only know Him in the Spirit.

Jesus then appears to His Disciples on Easter Sunday night. He wishes them peace and breathes on them (just as Yahweh breathed on Adam to make him a living creature). The Disciples were being made into a new creation. (Notice how in this Gospel, the Disciples receive the Holy Spirit on Easter Sunday and not on Pentecost as in the writings of Luke.)

One of the Disciples, Thomas, was not there that night. He wouldn't believe what the other Disciples were saying about Jesus until he could touch Jesus' wounds. When Jesus next appeared, He invited Thomas to touch those wounds.

The scene shows us two things. First of all, Jesus truly rose in the flesh. He had a body and was not a disembodied spirit. This was to reject the heresy of Docetism that denied that Jesus could have been both God and man.

This story also reminds us that we have to learn to trust (for we will not always see, but even then we can believe). How can we give our assent to things that we do not fully understand? Yet, aren't there many things in everyday life that we do not fully understand but believe (e.g., viruses, gravity, love). Faith is taking a leap of trust.

Chapter 21 opens with Jesus standing on the sea shore looking out at the Disciples who were fishing. They do not recognize Jesus, even when they get to shore. This is one of the times that we see that Jesus is somehow changed after the Resurrection. (The others are when Mary is in the garden and on the road to Emmaus.) Other times He is easily recognizable. This reminds us that with our resurrection we will be the same but changed.

The Disciples had been fishing all night long and they had not yet caught anything. Jesus tells them to try the other side of the boat and they caught a huge number of fish. This is extraordinary for one did not fish during the day on the Sea of Galilee because the surface water warmed up quickly and the fish swam deep. Fishermen could not catch them with their ancient shallow nets. Nevertheless, they caught 153 fish.

The Beloved Disciple, seeing with the eyes of faith, recognizes the Lord. Peter, impetuously, takes off his clothes and jumps in the water. When he gets to shore, Jesus serves a breakfast of fish and bread. This reminds us of the miraculous multiplication of loaves and fish. That time the bread was emphasized; this time it is the fish. The reason for the emphasis on the fish is that Jesus, the living bread, was standing in their midst, but also Jesus is calling them to be fishers of men. How successful will their catch be? They will catch 153 fish. According to some ancient Greek philosophers, this was the number of species of fish in the world. In other words, the Disciples were going to catch everyone in their nets of faith.

Jesus then asks Peter, "Do you love Me?" He answers that he does, and Jesus tells Peter to feed His lambs. Jesus asks him a second and third time, and Peter responds the same way.

Why did Jesus ask him the question three times? Part of the reason is that it allows Peter an opportunity to heal the hurt he caused by denying Jesus three times during the trial. The other reason has to do with Peter's responsibilities. Jesus is making Peter the shepherd, and thus giving him the role that He exercised as the Good Shepherd. This could possibly make Peter arrogant. Jesus reminds him that he is a sinner like the rest of us. This is similar to the old rite by which the Pope was crowned with a triple tiara. He was followed around by a Capuchin Franciscan who three times lit a clump of flax which burned like flash powder. He then whispered into the ear of the Pope, "*sic transit gloria mundi.*" This means, "so passes the glory of the world." Today we might say, "It's not going to last forever, so be careful."

After this profession of love, Peter asks Jesus, "What about him?" pointing at the Beloved. Jesus answers, "What's it to you if he is still alive when I return?" The text then makes it very clear that Jesus never said that he would be alive when He returned, only that it was none of his business if he were alive. Why is this particular saying included in the text? It seems to respond to some confusion that had arisen in the community. They thought that the Beloved would survive until the end of time. He has obviously died in the meantime and some in the community were scandalized because it seemed as if Jesus' promise had been broken, so the Gospel had to explain that this was all a misunderstanding. Jesus had never promised that the Beloved would survive until the end of the world.

Questions

1. What does it mean to say that John the Baptist was Jesus' best man?

2. Why was there so much wine at the Wedding Feast of Cana?

3. Do I serve other gods in my life, e.g. work, money, popularity, etc.?

4. When I do good things for others, am I sharing my love with them or am I just performing a task?

5. Do I truly think of myself as a brother or sister of Jesus? Do I see myself as another beloved disciple?

6. Is my faith like the Beloved's? Like Peter's? Like Mary Magdalene's? Like Thomas'?

Prayer

My Loving God, You are the source and the goal of my life and my love. You are my God and my all. May I live in Your love and share it with those who need it most.

Chapter 4

The Eucharist

The Eucharist in the Gospel of John

THE Gospel of John has a highly developed theology of the Sacrament of the Eucharist. We have already seen the account of the catch of 153 fish. This passage reminds us that the Eucharist calls us to the mission of sharing the Good News.

There are two other chapters in John which are eucharistic: chapter 6, the story of the miraculous multiplication of loaves and fish, and chapter 13, the account of the Last Supper.

If chapter 21 speaks of the call to mission in the Eucharist, chapter 6 speaks of its vertical dimension (that the Eucharist is truly the body and blood of Christ) and chapter 13 speaks of its horizontal dimension (that it is a call to service).

Furthermore, John has used an interesting structure called a chiasm to show how central the miraculous multiplication of loaves and fish is in this Gospel. A chiasm is a structure in which there is an odd number of sections. The first and last have similarities, the second and second last, etc. The most important section is found in the middle.

The first sign in this Gospel is the Wedding Feast of Cana. Jesus is there with His mother and the Disciples. He also mentions His hour (of glory). The last sign is the Cross. Again, we see Jesus, His mother, and His Beloved Disciple, and this is His hour of glory.

The second sign is the healing of the boy in Cana who is at the point of death. The second last sign is the raising of Lazarus, who had already died.

The third sign was the healing of the paralytic at the pool of Bethsaida. This occurs on the Sabbath and it gets them into trouble. The third last sign is the healing of the man born blind at the pool of Siloam which also occurs on the Sabbath and gets them both into trouble. The critical sign is the one found in the middle, the multiplication of loaves and fish found in chapter 6. This is the definition of what this community is all about: they are a people of the Eucharist.

The Multiplication of Loaves and Fish

THERE is at least one episode of the multiplication of loaves and fish in each of the Gospels. They all emphasize that this is an example of Jesus acting as the Good Shepherd. He has the crowd recline on the green grass (for in Psalm 23 the shepherd leads the flock to verdant pastures). After the multiplication, He walks across the waters and calms the sea (leading them to restful waters, again fulfilling Psalm 23).

In John's version, Jesus knows much more than He does in the other versions. He already knows what He is going to do even before He asks the Disciples about it.

Jesus receives five loaves of barley bread and two fish from a young boy. The very fact that this is barley bread and not wheat bread means that this boy was very poor. This was all he had to eat. Furthermore, five (loaves) and two (fish) equals seven. Even before Jesus had multiplied the loaves and fish, his gift was already perfect. Jesus takes it and makes it better by multiplying it.

Jesus gives thanks for these gifts. In the other Gospels, the evangelists use a perfectly good Greek word, "eudokeo," a word that simply means "to give thanks." John, on the other hand, used another word: "eucharistein." He wants us to realize that this is a pre-figuring of the Eucharist.

There are over 5,000 men present, not counting women or children (for they didn't count in those days). When they were all satisfied, Jesus ordered His Disciples to "gather up the fragments." This was actually a liturgical phrase used in the 1st century A.D. People reading the text would have recognized it as much as we recognize the phrase, "the breaking of the bread."

Some people interpret this miracle as a miracle of generosity. According to them, Jesus shared all the food He had, and the people saw this and shared all the food they had. This is a beautiful idea, but it is simply not what is being presented. This is a nature miracle, a sign that changes the rules of nature. If one failed to notice this, Jesus then goes out on the lake and takes a walk, another nature miracle.

Jesus crosses to the other side of the lake and many people follow Him. He challenges them as to why they were following Him. He accuses them of being there for free food.

In the first part of his discourse on the Bread of Life, Jesus presents Himself as wisdom incarnate. In the Old Testament, Lady Wisdom would instruct her followers. She nourished them with bread and wine which, if they ate them, would give them everlasting life. Jesus is Wisdom Whose teachings bring people to life eternal. Remember how the Samaritans considered Him to be the *Ta'eb*, the revealer of the secrets of God.

In verse 51c, the theme changes. Jesus says that the bread He is offering is His flesh for the life of the world. The word used for flesh is *"sarx."* In Greek, this is a very fleshy word. It means one's physical body. This would be comparable to a priest taking out a meat cleaver and cutting off his hand and inviting people to eat his flesh.

Jesus then says that besides eating His flesh, one also had to drink His blood. Jewish people do not consume blood. Kosher butchering, in fact, involves draining the animal's blood. It symbolizes life and belongs to God alone. It would be even more horrific for Jewish people to hear the phrase "drink his blood" than it would be to us.

Jesus then goes one step further and says one must "devour" His flesh (although this is often translated as "to eat"). We are supposed to be famished, desperate to eat it because otherwise we will not survive.

This passage clearly states that the Eucharist is the flesh and blood of Jesus. We don't understand this, but we believe it. The word "flesh" also reminds us of how much Jesus wants to be part of our lives. When is it that two flesh become one? In marriage! The only human action intimate enough to describe what happens between us and Jesus in the Eucharist is marriage. It is as if we were marrying our God.

At the end of the passage, we hear that some of the Disciples went away because they could not stand to hear these things. Jesus asked the twelve if they were going to go away too. Peter responds, "Lord, to whom shall we go? You have the words of everlasting life. We have come to believe that You are the holy one of God." This is the most positive picture of Peter in this Gospel, and yet even here, the Gospel takes a bit of a jab at the twelve for Jesus says that one of them was going to betray Him.

The Last Supper

THE account of the Last Supper is a bit unusual in this Gospel because it doesn't include any mention of Jesus taking bread and wine and calling it His body and His blood. In a sense, He has already done this in chapter 6 when He spoke about eating His flesh and drinking His blood. But it also seems as if He wants to present the horizontal dimension of the Eucharist: Jesus serving us and calling us to serve each other.

We hear that it was Passover time. Actually, if one reads the account carefully, it was the day before Passover. There were many pilgrims in Jerusalem at Passover time (250,000 pilgrims in a city that probably only had 60,000 inhabitants). There was not enough room for them to sleep inside the city walls. The rabbis decreed that they could sleep in the metropolitan area. Jesus, in fact, stayed in Bethany with Lazarus, Martha and Mary. Still, those coming to Jerusalem have to eat the Passover meal inside the city walls and there was not enough room for everyone, so the rabbis allowed them to anticipate the meal by one day. In the Gospel of John, this is what Jesus did. We know this because when He is arrested, the leaders of the Jews cannot enter Pilate's praetorium because they did not want to become unclean and not be able to eat the Passover meal that night. This means that Jesus actually died on preparation day. As they were nailing Him to the Cross, the paschal lambs were being slaughtered at the entrance to the temple. Bible scholars who have compared the Synoptic Gospel version (in which Passover begins on Holy Thursday night), with that contained in John have decided that the latter is probably correct.

We hear that Jesus knows that He is from the Father. That means that He knows that He is a God/man. What He is going to do at the Last Supper is not a denial of Who He is. It is an expression of His divinity. God is one Who loves and serves us to the end.

Jesus is doing this to give His Disciples an example of what they should now do. They were to love and serve each other. This is what it means to live in communion with each other.

Peter does not want to have his feet washed, and Jesus tells him that if he doesn't allow it, He will have no part with him. It is difficult to let others serve us. Most of us would much rather help others rather than ask them for help. There is a Yiddish saying that when a father helps a son, they both smile. When a son helps a father, they both cry. Peter must learn to allow himself to be served. Not asking for help when we need it is not only being arrogantly self-sufficient, it is also robbing from others the opportunity to do charity.

Peter misunderstands Jesus and asks Him to wash his hands and his head as well. Jesus answers that anyone who has had the "big bath" does not need to be washed all over, he only needs the "small washing." The big washing is Baptism; the small washing is the Sacrament of Reconciliation. Eucharist is one of the sacraments through which we receive forgiveness for our sins. It is the blood of Jesus poured out for the forgiveness of sins.

Questions

1. What is the meaning of the Eucharist in this Gospel?
2. Do I believe in the real presence of Jesus in the Eucharist?
3. Do I balance the vertical dimension of my faith with the horizontal?

Prayer

O holy banquet, in which Christ is received, the memory of His Passion is recalled, the soul is filled with grace, and a promise of future glory is given to us.

Chapter 5

New Life in Jesus and the Holy Spirit

Born of Water and the Spirit

IN chapter 3, Jesus had a dialogue with Nicodemus that addresses the other sacrament that we know that this community celebrated: Baptism.

Nicodemus is one of the elders of the Jews. He comes to Jesus by night for he is both afraid of revealing his faith in Jesus and he is also still in the dark for he does not yet know Jesus, the light of the world. There is a word play at the end of chapter 2 which gives us an insight into Nicodemus' character. Three times the word "man" is used to speak of those whom Jesus doesn't trust because He knows that their faith is superficial. We are then told at the beginning of chapter 3 that Nicodemus is a "man" from among the Pharisees. He is one of those whom Jesus does not trust.

At the end of chapter 7, Nicodemus appears a second time. The Pharisees are talking about what they should do with Jesus, and Nicodemus quotes the law saying that no one can be put to death without a trial. He is not really defending Jesus; he is defending the law. It is a lukewarm defense.

Finally, at the end of chapter 19, he and Joseph of Arimathea bury Jesus with great love. He is risking his life to bury a condemned criminal, but he is willing to take the risk.

In these three passages, we see Nicodemus grow in his faith. This is somewhat unusual because in ancient literature, characters are usually shown to be the way that they are from their earliest days. Our God, however, allows us to grow over time until we come to the fullness of faith.

The first time that Nicodemus speaks with Jesus, he says that he knows that Jesus is from God because no one can do what He is doing if God were not with Him. There is quite a bit of symbolic information here. First of all, Nicodemus says "he knows." There are two ways to say "to know" in Greek. One is superficial knowledge, and the other is a profound knowledge. When Nicodemus speaks about knowing, John uses the word meaning superficial knowledge. When Jesus says "to know," John uses the word that means profound knowledge.

Nicodemus says that he knows that Jesus is from God. Over and over again in the text, there is a debate about where Jesus is from. Here the Pharisees supposedly know where Jesus is from, but in chapter 9, the story of the man born blind, they claim that they do not know.

Nicodemus speaks of the signs that Jesus does. Jesus mistrusted those who followed Him because of signs. He felt that they were looking for a wonderworker. They did not realize that He wanted more than curiosity; He wanted trust and surrender.

Finally, Nicodemus says "unless God is with Him." The phrase "God with us" is Emmanuel, so the author is subtly declaring Jesus as the Emmanuel.

Jesus' response to Nicodemus is a bit strange for it seems to have nothing to do with what Nicodemus says. He says no one can see the kingdom of God unless he is born "anothen." This Greek word, "anothen," can either be translated as "again" or "from above." Jesus means "from above," but Nicodemus understands "again."

He asks Jesus how anyone can be born "again" when he is old, understanding Jesus' words in a totally material way. Jesus was trying to raise him to a spiritual understanding of what He was saying.

Jesus tells Nicodemus that he must be born of water and the spirit. Water refers to the Sacrament of Baptism, while Spirit refers to the Holy Spirit. It is not enough to go through a sacrament; one must also live that faith interiorly. Yet, it is also not enough to say that one belongs to God but does not live one's faith in an externally verifiable way.

Jesus then uses a word play. In Hebrew *(ruah)* and Greek *(pneuma)*, the same word can stand for spirit or wind or breath. He speaks of the spirit/wind blowing where it will. One cannot control the action of the Spirit. The Spirit is free and magnanimous and generous.

Nicodemus' final response to Jesus is, "How can this be?" His interventions have become shorter and shorter while those of Jesus have become longer and longer. In the face of God's wisdom and revelation, we come to realize how inadequate we are and we are eventually left saying, "How can this be?"

Jesus takes a little jab at Nicodemus. He says, "You are a teacher of Israel and you don't know these things." Nicodemus claimed that he "knew;" now he is being reminded how little he actually knows.

Jesus' discourses become even more mystical at this point. He speaks of knowing heavenly things. The Jewish people asked how we could possibly know the things of God when God was so far beyond our understanding. Jesus claims that He knows the things of God because He has come from God/from heaven.

He then speaks of the bronze serpent that Moses lifted up in the desert. The people had sinned, so Moses was told to make a bronze serpent which they could look upon to receive healing. He compares Himself to that object for He is the One Whom people could look upon when He is lifted up (on the cross) to receive life eternal.

God does not want to condemn us, but we can condemn ourselves. If we reject Jesus, we are already condemned (for by rejecting Jesus, we have to live without Him, and isn't that the worst curse one could call upon oneself).

The Story of Lazarus

WHAT does it mean to have eternal life? Jesus answers that question in the story of Lazarus. Lazarus, Mary and Martha were friends of Jesus. He stayed at their house when He went down to Jerusalem for the pilgrimage feasts. Mary and Martha sent word to Jesus in Galilee to tell Him that the one He loves was ill.

Even though Jesus loved Lazarus, He stayed where He was for the next few days. Oddly enough, it says "because" He loved him, He stayed there. How can this be an expression of love? If He really loved him, one would expect Him to rush to Lazarus' bedside to heal him. This is certainly what Mary and Martha expected, as will become clear when He eventually arrives in Bethany. But Jesus believed that it was more loving for Him not to be there and to let Lazarus die, for by his death, something very important was going to happen. If Lazarus died, then Jesus would raise him from the dead. If that happened, then the leaders of the Jews will try to stop Jesus from giving life and they will put Him to death.

A couple of days later, Jesus informs the Disciples that He is going to Lazarus who "has fallen asleep." Naturally, they interpret this as meaning that his fever had broken and he was sleeping it off. The only problem is that this is not what Jesus meant. He explains that Lazarus is dead and he is happy for their sake that he has died. Once again, this was so that they could witness the glory of God in His death on the cross.

Thomas then makes a bragging statement: "Come, let us die with Him!" Since we know that this same Thomas turns out to be "Doubting Thomas," we realize the irony of this statement.

Lazarus was four days dead when He arrived in Bethany. This is significant, for Jewish people believed that the soul stayed in the body for three days. If he was four days dead, then he was irretrievably dead.

Martha is the first person to meet Jesus. She greets Him with what can only be described as an accusation: "Lord, if You had been here, our brother would not have died." In modern English, we might say, "Where were you buddy?" Yet, she balances this statement with another: "But even now I believe that whatever You ask in God's name will be granted." Martha resembles many of us who give our assent of faith to God with one hand and pull it back with the other. She is like the man who has an epileptic son and of whom Jesus asks, "Do you believe?" His response is, "I do believe; help my unbelief."

Jesus tells Martha that her brother would rise again, and she answers that she knows that he will rise on the last day. Remember, not all Jews believed in the afterlife, but obviously Martha did.

Jesus then tells Martha, "I am the resurrection and the life." Notice, He is not saying, "I will give you the resurrection." He is saying that He is the Resurrection. If Jesus becomes part of one's life, then one is already in some way risen. This is what is called "realized eschatology." The term "eschatology" refers to the last things: death, judgment and one's eternal fate. Future eschatology means we have to wait for these things until our death.

Realized eschatology means that these things are already happening in the here and now. Heaven begins here on earth. The measure of heaven is how much Christ is the center of our lives and how much we are loving. St. Maximillian Kolbe was in the concentration camp of Auschwitz dying in a starvation bunker, but he sang hymns of praise and joy. He was in the most hellish place on the earth, and yet since he was one with God; he was already in heaven.

Martha responds with a significant profession of faith. She says that she believes that He is the Christ (the Messiah), the Son of God Who is coming into the world. This is almost the same profession that Peter makes in the other Gospels.

At this point, Mary arrives and greets Jesus. She says the exact same thing that Martha did, that if He had been there her brother would not have died. Like Martha, though, she also expresses her faith. She falls at His knees. One only kneels down to God, so she is expressing her faith that Jesus is God.

We hear that those around Jesus began to cry, and Jesus responds with anger. Who is He angry at? At Mary? At Martha? At the crowd who were crying? That would be hypocritical, for He cries Himself a few verses later. Maybe He is angry at death which has robbed Him of His beloved friend.

Jesus then cries. This is certainly a powerful scene in which we witness Jesus' humanity. It is a lesson for us even today: it is not a sin to grieve and mourn. We sometimes confuse our emotions with sinfulness. They are not wrong; they are simply part of life and a valid expression of who we are.

Jesus then asks to go to the tomb. Mary tries to talk Him out of it, even saying that there would be a stink if they were to open the tomb.

When they reach the tomb and open it, Jesus says a prayer that is obviously intended to show that everything that Jesus was doing, He was doing in the Father's name and authority.

When Lazarus comes out, Jesus orders that he be unbound. Jesus always does this; He frees us from all those things that imprison us.

What Jesus does to Lazarus is sometimes described as a resurrection, but it is not. It is a reanimation. A resurrection is when a person receives a glorified body that will never die again. Reanimation simply means that the person has come back to life but will one day die again.

One can ask what Lazarus got out of this. Martha and Mary got their brother back. Jesus gets His friend back. The Disciples get to see a miracle. But Lazarus is brought back to life only to have to die again some day. Furthermore, he comes back to life just in time to see his beloved friend Jesus crucified. Did he really want to be alive to see that? Yet maybe this is part of why Jesus brought him back to life. We share our suffering with our friends. Maybe Jesus wanted Lazarus to have a share in His suffering for He knew that by this, Lazarus would become the most loving person possible.

Questions

1. What is the significance of Baptism? Why are both water and the Spirit needed?
2. What does it mean when Jesus says, "I am the resurrection and the life?"

Prayer

Breathe Your spirit of life into my heart, O Lord. May I live each day of my life with a vitality and enthusiasm that is so profound that when I die, it will be to live in You forever.

Chapter 6

The Early Chapters

In the Beginning

WHEN Mark wrote his Gospel around 70 A.D., he began it with the story of Jesus' Baptism, the beginning of His public ministry. Unfortunately, some early heretics misinterpreted this passage as the moment when God adopted Jesus as His Son. For this reason, the next two Gospels written had infancy narratives. This showed that Jesus was already one with God when He was conceived. But soon enough that proved not to be enough, so the author of the fourth Gospel took it all the way back "to the beginning." There was never a time that Jesus was not God.

The way that the author phrases this hymn is obviously an allusion to wisdom passages in the Old Testament. Wisdom was present when God created the universe. She was, in fact, His architect and the blueprint of His project. This is all found in one way or another in this hymn, but the author did not use the word "wisdom," he used the word "word." Why? One possible reason is that in Greek, wisdom is a feminine word and Jesus was a male. But beyond this, there is also a rich theology of the word in Old Testament theology. By using this word, the author could make allusion to it and apply it to Jesus.

In Hebrew, "word" is *"dabar."* Yet, it means more than just a verbal expression. Each word makes real and present the reality it expresses. God speaks and it is so. Words are very powerful.

It also refers to God's saving plan. It is mysterious and inexpressible in human words. God reveals His Word to Jeremiah, but he and the other prophets must use many words to express these ideas (for their words always fall short).

There is also an Aramaic reason for using "the word." The name of God in the Old Testament was so sacred that it could not be said out loud. One has to substitute other words in its place. Most often people used the title "Adonay" which means "the Lord" in its place, but there were other words as well. One of the substitute words was the Aramaic word "memra" which meant "the word." So this author is saying that Jesus is the same as the Father for both can be called "the word."

Finally, there is a bit of Greek philosophy here. The Greek word for word is *"logos."* *Logos* is found in the philosophy of a Jewish Greek philosopher named Philo of Alexandria. He spoke of how God was so transcendent that He couldn't have anything to do with this material world. He therefore acted through a series of emanations which were successively more material and less spiritual. The main emanation in the work of creation was the *"logos."*

Thus, when John speaks of Jesus being the Word, he is making allusion to all of these ideas.

We hear that the Word was "with God." This is actually not the best translation of the Greek phrase here. It would be much more accurate to say that the Word was "towards God." It is as if the Father and the Son were always drawing closer together, but they never lost their individuality. Isn't this a beautiful image of heaven, that throughout eternity we will always be drawing closer and closer to God, falling more and more in love with Him.

We then hear that the Word was God. Jesus is and always was God together with the Father and the Spirit. Some non-Catholics translate this phrase as "the Word was divine." By this translation, they intend to say that Jesus was less than the Father and not God. The phrase actually could be translated either way, but when we look at the rest of the Gospel and how it speaks about Jesus, it becomes clear that the author of this Gospel considered Jesus to be God.

All of this material up to verse 14 refers to wisdom in Old Testament times. It came to Israel, but the people of Israel would not accept it (e.g., by rejecting the prophets). But those who do accept it will become children of God.

Verse 14 begins a treatment of Jesus and the Incarnation. The previous material could even have been Jewish, but from verse 14 on we are only talking about Jesus. We hear that the Word became flesh and He made His dwelling among us. As we saw when we spoke about the Eucharist, the word "flesh" is a very fleshy word. It refers to one's physical body. Jesus took on our human condition; He became one of us.

"He made His dwelling" is another of those phrases which has a number of symbolic meanings. It literally means "He pitched His tent among us." In the Old Testament, God manifested His presence in the Tent of Sanctuary. The Hebrew phrase for that manifestation, in fact, is *Shekinah* (a word that is related to the word for tent). John chooses a Greek word that sounds similar to these words but which also means to pitch a tent, thus speaking directly and indirectly of the same idea. John's ability to use these Hebrew and Greek ideas at the same time gives us a good indication of how brilliant this author was.

We also hear that Jesus' gift of self is so much more important than the gift given in the Old Testament. Moses gave us the law while Jesus gave us grace and truth. These were two attributes of God's promises in the Old Testament for he was filled with grace (love and mercy) and truth (always faithful to his promises). Jesus, in fact, gave us grace upon grace. This phrase is ambiguous and can be translated in one of three possible ways. It could mean that first there was one grace and then there was a second grace that built upon the first grace. Or it could mean that there was one grace and then a second grace which took the place of the first grace. Or a third possible translation is that there were tons and tons of grace. While most of us would be more comfortable with the first translation, that the Old Testament prepared for and was the foundation of the second covenant, it seems as if John actually intended the second translation (that Jesus replaced the promises and law and traditions of the first covenant).

In between all of these beautiful poetic ideas, we have already seen that there were prose verses that spoke about the role of John the Baptist. While the poetic ideas were probably borrowed from another author, the prose is certainly written by the author of this Gospel.

John's Disciples

WE have already seen that John the Baptist bore witness that Jesus was the Messiah. He calls Him the Lamb of God. This phrase has a double meaning in Aramaic (the language that

John the Baptist and Jesus both spoke). It could mean "Lamb of God" or it could mean "Servant of God" as in the Suffering Servant of God. Actually, both could have been intended, for as the Suffering Servant of God, Jesus died for our sins, slain as a lamb offered up in sacrifice.

The account doesn't actually report the Baptism of Jesus. John the Baptist tells us how it happened. The one difference between his own version and those found in the Synoptics is when he speaks of the Holy Spirit. In John, the Spirit descends upon Jesus in the form of a dove and remains upon Him.

Why is the Holy Spirit appearing in the form of a dove? The dove is the symbol for peace today, but in Old Testament times it was the symbol for love. In the Song of Songs, the lover calls the beloved a dove, saying that the lover has the eyes of a dove. The Holy Spirit is the Father's love for the Son and the Son's love for the Father. That Spirit remains upon Jesus to show us how we are called to remain in Him.

The next day, John again bore witness to Jesus calling Him the Lamb of God. Two of John's disciples heard him and went off to follow Jesus (a good example of what was said in chapter 3 that John must decrease while Jesus must increase). One of the Disciples is identified as Andrew while the other Disciple is never named. Most people believe that "the other Disciple" was the Beloved Disciple.

This would explain why this Gospel contains a number of themes that are also found in the writings of the Essene community at Qumran. They were celibate monks who were preparing for the great battle at the end of time between the sons of light and the sons of darkness. They were very dualistic, speaking of the two extremes of light and dark, goodness and sin, life and death, etc.

It is believed that John the Baptist spent time with the Essenes. This might be where he learned his practice of Baptism. The Essenes were very rigorous in their practice of ritual ablutions. If John the Baptist learned his theology there, then he would have passed it on to his disciples, and they could have passed it on to the community of the Beloved Disciple through "the other Disciple."

Peter and Nathanael

A NDREW, one of the two disciples, then found his brother Simon and brought him to Jesus. (Notice how this call of these disciples is different from that found in the Synoptics.) Jesus changes Simon's name to Peter (just as He does in Matthew's Gospel). "Peter" means "rock." In Matthew, Peter receives this name because he is the solid foundation for the Church. The reason why he receives this new name is not explained in John, but it might be a bit of a word play. Peter in Aramaic is "Cephas." This same word means "head" in Greek. Might this Gospel be saying that Peter is a bit hard headed. Throughout the Gospel he is certainly pictured as being terribly impetuous and even a bit foolish.

Jesus then calls Philip who informs Nathanael about Jesus. Nathanael's response when he hears that Philip believes that Jesus is the Messiah is a disparaging comment about Nazareth. It was, in fact, a dirt poor town, not the place that one would expect to be the home town of the Messiah.

His attitude changes significantly when Jesus greets him and calls him a true Israelite. This is an allusion to the story of Jacob. Jacob was a bit of a liar and cheat. While Genesis says that his name meant "the grasper" because he grasped the heel of his brother when he was born, Jeremiah says that his name really means "the deceiver." Yet, when he wrestled with God, he learned to be honest and sincere. That is when he received a new name, Israel. If Nathanael is a true Israelite, it means he is a Jewish scholar who seeks the truth. He is like Israel, not Jacob. Jesus also tells Nathanael that He saw him under the fig tree. This is the traditional place to study the Torah. When Nathanael professes his faith in Him, Jesus speaks of him seeing angels ascending and descending upon a ladder, once again a Jacob vision.

Questions

1. How could Jesus have existed even before He was born in Bethlehem?
2. Do I lead others to Christ as John's disciples did?

3. What word play is Jesus using when He calls Nathanael a true "Israelite"?

Prayer

Call me, O Lord, to follow You unreservedly. Teach me Your ways and guide me in Your steps.

Chapter 7

Jesus' Teachings

The Good Shepherd

IN chapter 10, we see Jesus use another Old Testament theme to describe His mission. A number of prophets around the time of the Babylonian exile used the image of the shepherd as the ideal for their kings. The kings of Israel and Judah had been bad, and the prophets were hoping for a king who might shepherd the people of God. God therefore swore to remove them and replace them either with honest shepherds or with Himself.

Ezekiel's version of this prophesy was read at the Feast of the Dedication (Chanukah) each year. Jesus, Who went to that feast with His Disciples, heard the reading and applied it to Himself. He was not a mercenary; He was the Good Shepherd Who was willing to die for His sheep (and He later calls Himself the sheepgate as well). He knows His sheep by name and they recognize His voice (which we see when Mary Magdalene recognizes His voice).

Jesus is the Good Shepherd. He passes on that responsibility to Peter in chapter 21 when Jesus asks Peter to feed His sheep.

The Last Supper Discourse

IN the ancient world, the last words or discourse of an important figure were considered to be the most important words of that person's life, e.g. Socrates' last words to his disciples. Luke recognizes this for he has Jesus give His Disciples last minute instructions on how they were to behave (not lording it over those in their care).

The discourse in John is extensive. It goes from the beginning of chapter 14 til the end of chapter 17. We have already seen how the discourse might have originally ended at the end of chapter 14. The material from the beginning of chapter 15 until the end of chapter 17 was probably added a little later.

Did Jesus say all these things at the Last Supper or were these speeches that were given all throughout His ministry and collected and put here to give them added importance? This would be similar to what Matthew did when he collected the teachings of Jesus and put them into five major sections of discourse.

Some scholars would go one step further. They would claim that they are remembrances of what Jesus said but not the exact words. They might even have been built upon an accurate skeleton of what Jesus said by some preacher in the community.

The Paraclete

ONE of the instructions from the Last Supper Discourse is about the "Paraclete." This is actually the English form of a Greek word. This particular word is very difficult to translate for it has so many possible meanings. It could mean counselor (like a royal counselor) or consoler (someone who comforts a person in trouble) or advocate (like a lawyer). Many Bibles, in fact, simply leave the word "Paraclete" so that it can hint at all of these possible meanings.

Even though the Holy Spirit is mentioned quite often in the New Testament, we do not have a theology of the Holy Spirit except for two passages. In 1 Corinthians we hear that the Holy Spirit acts in God as our spirit acts within us. Then we have these passages in John: 14:16ff.26; 15:26; 16:6ff.

In these verses, we first of all hear that the Paraclete is "another advocate." Jesus is the first advocate, the *"go'el."* This was the relative in Jewish society who would take one's part when no one else would. If one were going to lose one's property because of debts, the *go'el* would lend money without interest. If someone killed a person, the *go'el* would seek blood vengeance. If one died without having children, then one's *go'el* married the widow.

Jesus is our *go'el.* He takes our part when no one else will. He defends us against our worst enemies: sin, hate, fear, death, etc. He even takes our part when we sin against ourselves, so in this sense He is closer to us than our own heart.

The Holy Spirit is "another" *go'el.* The Spirit now takes our part. We certainly see this in the Sacrament of Reconciliation for the Spirit brings us forgiveness of our sins.

When do the Father and the Son send the Holy Spirit? We have already seen that Jesus breathes on the disciples on the evening of Easter Sunday. In Luke's writings, Mary and the Apostles receive the gift of the Holy Spirit on Pentecost Sunday. Which is it? Actually both are somehow true. John was a mystic. For mystics, time is not important. Once we enter the Paschal Mystery, time as we know it has passed away. We have entered into eternity. We have a sense of this when we celebrate the Mass (for we are at the Last Supper, the Cross, and the Resurrection). We also have a sense of this during the Holy Triduum, the days running from Holy Thursday until the Easter Vigil. These days are all one event, a glimpse into eternity.

Luke, on the other hand, was a historian. For him, time was very important. Therefore we see the forty days up to the Ascension and the fifty days up to Pentecost.

We hear that the world would not accept the Paraclete. This is part of the dualism of the Gospel. The world is contrasted with the Spirit. The world is corrupt and immoral. This was a Greek philosophical idea, which is why it was so unusual that this same Gospel also speaks of Jesus becoming flesh.

This Spirit will dwell within us and make us one with Jesus and the Father. The Spirit's love binds the Father to the Son and them to us. Paul says that the Spirit dwells in our hearts and reminds us that God is Abba. If someone were to ask us what we would most want God to say to us, most of us would respond, "I love you." Where did that hope come from? Did we make it up? No! It is the Spirit who placed that hope in our hearts, for God is the answer to our most profound hopes for the Spirit made us hope for those things.

The Spirit will teach us (14:26) and help us to remember. Jesus taught us here on earth, but our minds cannot possibly comprehend all the mysteries of God. We need the Holy Spirit to continue to instruct us and help us understand the meaning of what Jesus taught us about God. Furthermore, the Spirit helps us to remember (both the revelation of God and how God acts in our lives, for we often only see God's fingerprints in hindsight).

The Holy Spirit is the Spirit of truth (15:26). There is an absolute truth, even if at times it is difficult for us to discern it in our changeable world. At times, in fact, we can't even know the truth if it is not first revealed to us by God.

The Spirit also bears witness to Jesus (15:26). The Spirit speaks in our hearts, revealing Who Jesus is. We come to the faith, in fact, because the Spirit leads us to believe. This makes sense, for faith is both a gift and an act of trust. When we profess our faith in the creed, we say, "I believe in God." This is like saying, "God, I believe in You; I trust You." How can we trust others if we have not learned to trust because we were loved by God. This is what the First Letter of John says when it says that love does not mean that we have loved God as much as God has loved us first.

In 16:9 we hear that the Spirit speaks to us about sin. In this Gospel, the only sin is not to believe in the only Son of God. The Spirit gives witness that Jesus is the Christ, so anyone who doesn't believe that Jesus is the Christ is not listening to the Spirit and thus not living in God's love.

The Spirit gives witness concerning righteousness. Jesus is the righteous one Who teaches us the ways of God, how to be righteous ourselves. The Spirit bears witness that Jesus and the Father are one; therefore what He taught is absolutely true.

The Spirit gives witness concerning judgment. The Spirit is the Spirit of truth and love. The prince of this world (Satan) is the Father of Lies and the Prince of Hate. The Spirit gives witness to the defeat of sin and hate and lies.

Finally, the Spirit glorifies Jesus. Remember, in this Gospel, glory is the outpouring of love. Jesus glorifies the Father because He lovingly does that which the Father wills. He does not consider it humiliation to submit to the Father's will. He considers it the fulfillment of His desire to be the most loving person possible. The same is true of the Holy Spirit. The Spirit does not seek self-aggrandizement. The Spirit does not seek recognition. The Spirit points to the Father and the Son and praises them.

Questions

1. What does the image of Christ being the Good Shepherd teach us about our relationship with Him?

2. Do I say the really important things to those whom I love just as Jesus did at the Last Supper?

3. What does this Gospel teach us about the Holy Spirit?

Prayer

The Lord is my shepherd,
I shall not want.
He makes me lie down in green pastures,
He leads me to tranquil streams.

Conclusion:
Who Wrote What?

Who Wrote This Gospel?

A CCORDING to tradition, this Gospel, the Letters of John and the Book of Revelation were all written by John, the son of Zebedee. Tradition tells us that he is the Beloved Disciple, the hero of this Gospel. His name is never mentioned in the Gospel, according to some, because of his great humility.

There are some difficulties with this theory. First of all, the geography is problematic. John, the son of Zebedee, came from Galilee (remember, he was a fisherman on the Sea of Galilee). Yet, whenever the geography of Galilee is mentioned, it is not all that accurate. On the other hand, when the geography of Jerusalem is mentioned, it is highly accurate. There are some references to places in Jerusalem that only appear in this Gospel which are nevertheless historic, e.g., the pool of Bethsaida (ch. 6). This pool was called the pool of the five porticoes and it was associated with healing. Until this century, no one knew where it was. Archaeologists have now discovered a pool with five porticoes (four around the edge and one through the middle to divide the man's portion from the woman's portion) that is next door to a pagan temple dedicated to healing. John's knowledge of Jerusalem is thus, at times, more accurate than that of the other Gospels. This would seem to mean that the source of this Gospel is someone from Jerusalem and not from Galilee.

A second problem is that the Greek in this Gospel is very good and there are times that there is Greek philosophy in it. How many Galilean fishermen would be able to write this type of Gospel? A possible response to this problem is that maybe it was actually written by a disciple of the Beloved Disciple who was better educated. There is even a hint of this in chapter 21 when the author speaks about the Beloved in the third person, as if the author and the Beloved are two different people.

A third problem is how this Gospel treats Apostles. The Gospel never once uses the word apostle (almost as if it is a dirty word). There is no list of the twelve Apostles. Whenever one of them appears, they seem to come across poorly. The Beloved, on the other hand, comes across very well in the Gospel. Why would John, one of the Apostles, treat his fellow Apostles so disrespectfully.

Finally, the Beloved can enter the High Priest's house on the night of Jesus' trial. How would a fisherman have such access?

These difficulties are daunting, but they are not absolute. If one wants to continue to believe that John is the Beloved, fine!

If it was not John, though, who could it be? A few scholars have suggested that it might have been Lazarus. He is called beloved by Jesus. He lives near Jerusalem. He also seems to have been wealthy (for he was able to host Jesus and the Disciples during pilgrimage festivals. None of this, of course, can be proven.

Why would the ancients have attributed this Gospel to John, the son of Zebedee? It could very well be because the portrayal of Jesus in this Gospel is so elevated. Two of the early heresies in the Church were Gnosticism and Docetism, both of which denied the humanity of Jesus. These heresies, in fact, wrote commentaries upon the Gospel of John, as if it were one of their own works. Was the Christology so high that it might be interpreted as heretical?

There are two things that saved this Gospel. First of all, it was attributed to John, the son of Zebedee, one of the great three Apostles. It therefore had important apostolic authority. It was not uncommon in ancient times to attribute a work to an important author. This might have been what happened with the Letter to the Hebrews which for centuries was attributed to Paul but was most probably not written by him.

The other thing that saved this Gospel was the beginning of the First Letter of John. It begins, "that which we heard from the beginning." By using the phrase "from the beginning," the author of this letter is tying it to the Gospel which also begins, "In the beginning." In the Gospel, this phrase was used to speak of the eternal pre-existence of the Son. In the First Letter of John, the phrase is used to speak of the beginning of their faith in Jesus. The author speaks of hearing and seeing and touching Jesus. He was truly born in the flesh. This letter gave the community a non-heretical way of interpreting the Gospel.

Thus, the Gospel was saved for the community and for this we are most grateful. It is a beautiful, symbolic Gospel that invites us to fall in love with God again. We are all intended to be the Beloved.

What About John's Other Writings?

DID the author of this Gospel also write the three letters of John? When one examines the theology and vocabulary of the Gospel and the Letters, one finds that they are significantly different. It is very difficult to believe that the author of the Gospel is the same as the author of the three letters (although all three of these letters could have been written by the same author).

The Book of Revelation states that it was written by "John." All apocalyptic books were written under a pseudonym, so the very fact that it states that it was written by John means that it wasn't. Its vocabulary and theology are also different from both the Gospel and the letters. It was probably written by someone else.

Having said this, I must admit that I have a running nightmare that I reach the Pearly Gates and John, the son of Zebedee, is standing there with five scrolls upon which are written the Gospel, the letters and the Book of Revelation, and he is hitting me over the head saying, "What do you mean that I didn't write these?"

Questions

1. Who wrote this Gospel?
2. Who wrote the Letters of John and the Book of Revelation?

Prayer

St. John, pray for us.

THE MIRACLES OF JESUS DURING HIS PUBLIC LIFE

Water Made Wine: Jn 2:1-11.
The Royal Official's Son: Jn 4:46-54.
The Catch of Fishes: Lk 5:1-11.
The Cure of a Demoniac: Mk 1:23-28; Lk 4:33-37.
Peter's Mother-in-law: Mt 8:14-15; Mk 1:29-31; Lk 4:38-39.
The Leper: Mt 8:1-4; Mk 1:40-45; Lk 5:12-19.
The Paralytic at Capernaum: Mt 9:1-8; Mk 2:1-12; Lk 5:18-26.
The Cure at Bethesda: Jn 5:1-15.
The Man with a Shriveled Hand: Mt 12:9-13; Mk 3:1-6; Lk 6:6-11.
The Centurion's Servant: Mt 8:5-13; Lk 7:1-10.
The Widow's Son: Lk 7:11-17.
The Blind and Dumb Demoniac: Mt 12:22.
Calming of the Storm: Mt 8:23-27; Mk 4:35-41; Lk 8:22-25.
Expulsion of the Demons in Gadara: Mt 8:29-34; Mk 5:1-20; Lk 8:26-39.
Jairus' Daughter: Mt 9:18-26; Mk 5:21-43; Lk 8:40-56.
The Woman in the Crowd: Mt 9:20-22; Mk 5:24-34; Lk 8:43-48.
Two Blind Men: Mt 9:27-31.

The Possessed Mute: Mt 9:32-34.
Five Thousand Fed: Mt 14:13-21; Mk 6:34-44; Lk 9:12-17; Jn 6:1-15.
Jesus Walks on the Water: Mt 14:22; Mk 6:45-52; Jn 6:16-21.
The Canaanite Woman: Mt 15:21-28; Mk 7:24-30.
Healing of a Deaf-Mute: Mk 7:31-37.
Four Thousand Fed: Mt 15:32-38; Mk 8:1-9.
The Blind Man at Bethsaida: Mk 8:22.
A Possessed Boy: Mt 17:14-21; Mk 9:13-28; Lk 9:37-43.
The Temple Tax Provided: Mt 17:23-26.
The Man Born Blind: Jn 9:1-38.
The Crippled, Blind and Mute: Mt 15:29.
A Woman Cured: Lk 13:10-17.
The Raising of Lazarus: Jn 11:1-44.
The Man with the Dropsy: Lk 14:1-6.
Ten Lepers: Lk 17:11-19.
The Blind Men at Jericho: Mt 20:29-34; Mk 10:46-52; Lk 18:35-43.
The Fig Tree Cursed: Mt 21:18-22; Mk 11:12-14.
The Servant's Ear Healed: Lk 22:49-51.
The Catch of Fishes: Jn 21:1-14.

THE PRINCIPAL PARABLES OF JESUS

Children, The Wayward, Mt 11:16-19; Lk 7:31-35.
Debtors, The Two, Lk 7:41-42.
Fig Tree, A Sign of Summer, Mt 24:32-35; Mk 13:28f; Lk 21:29-31.
Fig Tree, The Barren, Lk 13:6-9.
Judge, The Corrupt, Lk 18:1-8.
Kingdom, A Divided, Mt 12:25-27; Mk 3:23-26; Lk 11:17f.
Laborers in the Vineyard, Mt 20:1-16.
Merciless Official, The, Lk 18:21-35.
Mustard Seed and the Leaven, Mt 13:31f; Mk 4:30-32; Lk 13:18f.
Net, Parable of the, Mt 13:47-50.
Pharisee and the Tax Collector, Lk 18:9-14.
Rich Man and Lazarus, Lk 16:19-31.
Rich Man, The Foolish, Lk 12:16-21.
Samaritan, The Good, Lk 10:29-37.
Seat, The Lowest, Lk 14:7-14.
Seed, The, Mt 13:3-23; Mk 4:3-20; Lk 8:4-15.
Seed, The Growing, Mk 4:26-29.

Servant, The Faithful and the Worthless, Mt 24:45-51; Lk 12:42-48.
Servants, The Useless, Lk 17:7-10.
Sheep, The Straying, Mt 18:12-14; Lk 15:3-7.
Shepherd, The Good, Jn 10:1-21.
Silver Pieces, The, Mt 25:14-30.
Son, The Prodigal, Lk 15:11-32.
Sons, The Two, Mt 21:28-32.
Sums of Money, Parable of, Lk 19:11-27.
Tenants, The, Mt 21:33-46; Mk 12:1-12; Lk 20:9-19.
Treasure and the Pearl, Mt 13:44-46.
Vigilance, Exhortation to, Mt 24:43f; Lk 12:39f.
Vine, and the Branches, The, Jn 15:1-17.
Watchfulness, The Need for, Mk 13:34-37; Lk 12:36-38.
Wedding Banquet, The, Mt 22:1-14; Lk 14:16-24.
Weeds, The, Mt 13:24-30.
Wily Manager, The, Lk 16:1-13.
Yeast, The, Mt 13:33.